TRAVELS IN
SAN
FRANCISCO

Also by Herbert Gold

Novels

Short Stories and Essays

Memoir

Reportage

TRAVELS IN SAN FRANCISCO

Herbert Gold

ARCADE PUBLISHING • NEW YORK

Little, Brown and Company

FIRST EDITION

Photographs by Gene Anthony

The pieces in this book originally appeared,
in somewhat different form, in the *Washington Post,
Playboy,* the *San Francisco Chronicle,* and *San Francisco Focus.*

Library of Congress Cataloging-in-Publication Data

Gold, Herbert, 1924–
    Travels in San Francisco / Herbert Gold. — 1st ed.
    p. cm.
    ISBN 1-55970-017-3
    1. San Francisco (Calif.) — Fiction. 2. San Francisco (Calif.) —
Description. I. Title.
PS3557.O34T74 1990
813'.54 — dc20   89-15095
                                              CIP

Published in the United States by Arcade Publishing, Inc., New York,
a Little, Brown company.

10 9 8 7 6 5 4 3 2 1

FG

Designed by Jacques Chazaud

*Published simultaneously in Canada
by Little, Brown & Company (Canada) Limited*

PRINTED IN THE UNITED STATES OF AMERICA

For Rita and Rex, fellow walkers,
and for Leo,
who can never resist a spare-changer

Contents

Contents

Photographs follow page 88

TRAVELS IN SAN FRANCISCO

Introduction
San Francisco as Part
of the Real World

Vigilantes to Dr. Lovejoy, a San Francisco con man:
"Is there anything you'd like to say before you're hung?"

Dr. Lovejoy: "Not at this time."

San Francisco is famous
for running a hundred-year-old operetta for the entertainment of itself, visiting sailors, and other tourists and
conventioneers. The sets include North Beach (Italian
jollity and cappuccino), the Tenderloin (ambisexual
lower depths), Chinatown (souvenirs, restaurants, and
an occasional gang rumble), Fisherman's Wharf (seafood, sea smells, and bongo players), the Haight-
Ashbury (a now-gentrified counterculture), the Castro
(Shangri-la for homosexuals), Nob, Russian, and Telegraph hills (worn elegance), Pacific Heights and Union
Street (spanking-bright elegance and singles shopping);

3

the characters include beatniks, hippies, ethnics of black, brown, yellow, and pink hues, and a large supporting cast of prospering runaways from less clement climes. There are also the Old Families, who have been here more than twenty minutes and have made their money in banking, insurance, mining, railways, land, or politics. Or in the manufacture of jeans. There are the cute and the less cute crazies. San Francisco is America's Pigalle and Saint-Germain-des-Prés, if not its Paris.

The above exaggerations are not fair to the case, of course, any more than it's fair to say that Washington, DC, is merely government. But it's also part of the truth, isn't it?

A walking town, blessedly limited and cleansed by the bay and ocean, San Francisco is also America's last great metropolitan village. It is a place to be explained, like the blind man defining an elephant — different wherever you happen to touch it. Let us stipulate, before dealing in its oddnesses, that it is also a city like any other middle-American place — a union town, a place of residential neighborhoods and watered gardens and kids playing, the Richmond, Sunset, Mission, and Noe Valley districts. While middle- and working-class people who attend PTA meetings occupy most of the city, the few blocks along Valencia that form a kind of lesbian nation are more likely to attract attention. And perhaps this is as it should be, since exceptional laboratories and resorts are appropriate for visitors, who, after all, are seeking to break out and Make It New, temporarily.

San Francisco's provincial pride and self-importance are reminiscent of other places with a historical vision

4

of themselves, such as Boston, Chicago, or New Orleans. Yet nobody came first; it was a place of a few hundred frontiersmen until the Gold Rush, a mere 140 years ago. I once heard the publisher of the *San Francisco Examiner*, the former flagship of the Hearst newspapers — now struggling against the mighty *Chronicle*, an entertaining daily magazine — praise Kenneth Rexroth during a testimonial dinner to the distinguished old literary man: "He is a great poet, a great critic, and one of the *San Francisco Examiner*'s finest columnists." Self-reference is one of San Francisco's habits, like the beautiful woman who has a few nagging doubts. A front-page story in the *Chronicle* — on a day when sieges of the British and Libyan embassies in London and Tripoli, mining of Nicaraguan ports, political campaigns, perturbations in the economy, and the unbalanced budget were the big news in other newspapers — concerned the crusade by Warren Hinckle to change the city song from Tony Bennett's "I Left My Heart in San Francisco" to the "San Francisco" made famous by Jeanette MacDonald in a Clark Gable earthquake movie. The first sounds like a ditty about an item forgotten in a hotel room, but the second reminds people of the earthquake past and, more important, to come.

This is not an unusual controversy for the *San Francisco Chronicle*, which through the years has served the region by exposing the defects of restaurant coffee, has explored the local beatnik and hippie philosophies, and has featured the columnist Herb Caen's witty and bemused view of the scene for more than fifty years. A typical *Chronicle* lead might read: "Ten thousand drug-crazed, bottle-wielding hippies failed to appear this morning at City Hall."

Boxes selling the *New York Times, USA Today,* the *Wall Street Journal,* and other newspapers have been implanted all over town, but the proud *Chronicle* retains a firm grip on the spirit of the place.

Recently I met an immigrant to San Francisco, a former editor of *Harper's Bazaar* who found herself at this frontier after a divorce. Knowing herself to be canny, shrewd, disabused, très East Coast, she was properly suspicious of the trendy Bay Area. "I hate all these cults and fads," she said, "est, Dianetics, Bubba Free John, Synanon, Muktananda, Eckankar, Sri Rajneesh, Baba Ram Dass, all those phonies — you know?"

"I know."

She tapped a pencil to her exquisite nose (a little more exquisite than the one she used to have). She was ready to share something with me. "Only one of those groups is any good. It's my Tuesday evening Affluence Visualization Seminar. I used to have a problem about getting rich, really visualizing it, you know, so I was stuck at the bourgeois level. I didn't appreciate myself, but now I'm up for it and it's happening."

"You mean your class helps you to get along with being rich or it helps you to get money?"

"Both. My problem was both. It was my anima. Affluence Visualization is a combination of the best in Arica, Zen, Jung, and our leader's own discoveries about how you really see it in your own heart and mind — he's beautiful. A karma like you wouldn't believe. Used to be a super ad man, but he dropped out because he really visualized being a tycoon in the field of helping people."

The lady was overcome by the mood of the Bay Area — define yourself, make yourself whatever you want — but she is fulfilling her dream with a little Gesture for Success business, a boutique-improvement enterprise. Trendiness is a persistent trend in this climate where it is forever springtime. When I came out to live in San Francisco thirty years ago, I discovered that you never had to wonder whether or not to open or shut the window — the weather was okay. You didn't have to rush out to enjoy a good day; most days are good. It was nice to work in a place where the climate is a friend. There are enough adversaries elsewhere in the world.

But perhaps ease has a price in the emphasis on food, comfort, style, and making out okay. A bookstore owner reports that a San Francisco matron, planning a trip to Europe, came in to ask for George Orwell's *Dining Out in Paris and London*. A high-school girl in a literature class, studying Shakespeare's *Romeo and Juliet*, wrote in her paper that Juliet spoke to Romeo from her "deck." A perhaps apocryphal advertisement on behalf of a progressive couple: "Seek to adopt a gay baby."

There are rent-a-dream businesses, cars for that special date, maybe dates for that special car. Celebrities are for lease. A couple I know stages parties with themes for people who want to live out their fantasies. In my jeans and boots I attended a beatnik party for a violinist celebrating his sixtieth birthday: he remembered that he was young and full of vibrato in the fifties. Other themes offered: first-class ocean liner, tennis-

7

anyone, and, of course, that quaint old standby — the orgy. There is also a lawyer who can make you into a fairly genuine bank president for a small fee. He sets up the papers; you now own a bank, or at least a postal deposit box with a banklike name, on some charming Caribbean island.

All of this smoke and fume exists in every American place, even in my hometown of Cleveland — where I find a mini–San Francisco in the Coventry–Euclid Heights Boulevard neighborhood — but the concentration is richer here. A few people jog in Cleveland; a horde of running executives stake out their territory in the City and County of San Francisco. They fight traffic instead of doing lunch downtown during the midday. They streak past tourists, delivery trucks, outdoor food wagons, bicyclists with propellers on their cute messengers' heads. Old San Francisco is the backdrop for these aerobic anticholesterol achievers, loping and roaming past the new high-rise sites, working out their primeval animal rebirth. During the sunny or foggy business days of the city, it's an inspiring vision of optimism. New office suites are being built with showers. The rest of us are playing squash or racquetball.

I used to describe the street life of San Francisco as a carnival. Operetta now seems more appropriate, although there are some hazards in street crime, transvestite hookers, a diverse outpatient population — junkies, geriatrics, alcoholics, recent immigrants from Southeast Asia, halfway-house lodgers, sexual outlaws, motorcycle and leather people — and even a few bohemians stacked among the porn houses, racketing bars, used book and record and clothing and food stores in the Tenderloin, near several of the city's major hotels. A few days ago, walking to the Press Club, I saw a man waving his wallet, out of which money was leaking, at a stiletto-heeled person who was either a man or a woman: "Hey! You dropped your hook!"

As I passed him, he was muttering compassionately, "A hooker needs her hook."

Yet even the Tenderloin is a neighborhood with a certain dead-end animation and energy. Funky psychedelic murals, like prehistoric cave paintings, are fading into history in stores that used to sell "paraphernalia" and now house bewildered Southeast Asian tribespeople. Jane Jacobs, in her book *The Death and Life of Great American Cities*, listed San Francisco's North Beach as one of the great American neighborhoods, along with Greenwich Village and a part of Boston that has been mostly redeveloped since. North Beach, despite topless dancing, still carries on the tradition of the Barbary Coast. But the long-running operetta has also spawned new strolling and eating-out and café-sitting neighborhoods all over this town that is so energetically devoted to pleasure: Russian Hill has cafés, and Clement has become an auxiliary Chinatown, and Potrero Hill has leaned a small bohemia against its Greek, Thai, and White Russian community. The Haight has revived; there are espresso machines and bookshops out near the various art cinemas on Irving and Chestnut and Union streets. Discretionary income, time, and energy are among the deals that come with forever-springtime. Not many people are artists and philosophers, yet the cafés and streets seem to be full of them. Those who like the town a lot (of whom I am usually one) might describe it as a medieval city with marketplaces and life expended in raucous public, a Mediterranean port with a history — albeit a short one — enclaves of defined neighborhoods, variety, fun, sunlight, fog. Those who like the city less (of whom I am also occasionally one) might turn up their judgment at the tourist-thirst of some of the gentrified spaces, the occasional look of a mere outdoor shopping mall crowded with cute, promotional, profitable. Most of the time, the relative avoidance of slavery to the automobile, the imprisonment within watery boundaries, means that San Francisco avoids the look of an agglomerated megalopolis. As Spinoza said, freedom consists in knowing what the limits are. There may be crazies in the streets, but at least the streets are not barren freeways. The air is swept by the winds through the Golden Gate. The smog is beyond the hills and over there — across the bay in Oakland.

The city tends to regenerate itself and fight back. Freeway revolts, high-rise ordinances, antismoking campaigns don't always triumph, but sometimes they do. Change is not always for the worse. Take, for example, the old Haight-Ashbury, the land of acid dreams during the Summer of Love. Has it settled back into its prehistory of an easygoing San Francisco neighborhood, or kept its sad postrevolutionary role as America's first teenage slum, a troubled and dangerous ghetto, or has it been gentrified into still another Old Town, Union Street, Shopping Mall Ninetiesland?

None of the above. The Haight has not been redeemed entirely, but it is becoming one of the great, slightly eccentric, yet attractive all-American neighborhoods — a mixture of Orientals, blacks, gays, young families, and students on the old foundation of working-class San Francisco. During the beatnik era of North Beach, Bunny Simon — a stately, slow-moving, and courtly Creole gentleman from New Orleans — presided over a talk-and-poetry hangout called the Anxious Asp. The North Beach saloon establishment didn't take to a man of color running a bar on its turf and he was forced out. Then Bunny Simon parked his wife's Rolls-Royce, a gift from him in honor of her Creole cooking, in front of his popular bar on Haight Street. . . . The Anxious Asp returns! Besides presiding over this establishment, he was writing a book. Sometimes I dropped in to discuss it with him, along with one of his favorite novelists, Ernest Gaines, author of the prizewinning novel and film *The Autobiography of Miss Jane Pittman.* Everything changes; yet some things remain the same. For a while.

Many things are better in the Haight. During the period of litter, dope, and turmoil, the Haight-Ashbury shared with New York's East Village a dubious distinction: middle-class wrack and ruin. The neighborhood organized; business people and residents dug in. Now it is one of the truly integrated neighborhoods, every which way — black and white, gay and straight, student and elderly, single and familied, poor and up-up-upwardly mobile. If not a Gold Coast Old Town, it's a Credit Coast Newville. The revived district has taken its place as a strolling, dining, shopping, café-sitting, moderately levelheaded — but only moderately — cappuccino, croissant, quiche, book-and-record, Tiffany glass, health emporium, exercise studio, urban settlement. Some of the barbershops are not styling salons. There may be more Hunan cooking than is absolutely required, but there are also corner groceries. Less chic than Union Street or downtown San Francisco, the gentry of the Haight retain just a soupçon of laidback from ancient flower times.

Recently I spoke with a young woman at the Red Victorian Cinema who said she used to be a street person, a dropout, but now she has straightened out her life and is going back to school to get her master's degree. "In what subject?" I asked.

"Holistics and Astrology," she said.

Since flaky remains a fact of life — although life is real and earnest, here as everywhere — it's better to accept the special atmosphere. Asked the word for a body of water entirely surrounded by land, a Marin County child answered, "Hot tub?" The proprietor of Fabulous Faces offers "caviar facials." After the dancer wife of a pianist ran off briefly with one of his musician friends, the couple rented a hall to perform a dance celebrating the recementing of their marital bonds. The performance had three parts: "Fugue," "Interlude," and "Return." The pianist and the dancer took joint bows to mild applause and lived happily forever afterward, or at least until the next month and the fourth part: "Dissolution."

A large percentage of the population of San Francisco lives alone — divorced or never married or gay or just young and, like Dick Whittington, come to the great city to fulfill the imperatives of hope and desire. The streets form a kind of maxi-family for those uprooted from traditional families. For the visitor, San Francisco can be a way of testing another sometimes humorous, sometimes sensual, sometimes merely wasteful way of living. Along with the new biotechnology and computer industries in the Bay Area, a village economy, a financial concentration, San Francisco is the locale for its unique celebration of itself. Those who come to visit are welcome to join the chorus during intervals between their own recitatives concerning the future of America.

Morning Starter

Get up and go — the best philosophy for jump-starting the metabolism.

For a portion of the population unrecorded in the latest census data, breakfast at home is an unthinkable violation of proper procedure. To wake out of the uneasy warmth and persuade the blood to move, the brain to click in, requires an outing, a bit of walk, a sniff of unbreathed air, fruit or eggs or oatmeal or hotcakes, a lot of coffee. The soul requires sampling the variously freshened scents of early morning and the emanations of anonymous other breakfasters. Nothing better can compensate for the abandonment of dreamland.

14

I've liked, and still like, Le Petit Café on Russian Hill and Just Desserts in the Marina, but due to the mysteries of jet lag and metabolism, I seem to be getting up earlier and earlier. Something canine in me takes dawn as the signal to start salivating. Many places don't open until 7:30 AM. Even after a bit of hiking, I've found myself lurking outside, warming myself in a neighborhood launderette, interrupted in the rhythms of correct procedure. I want my breakfast *now*.

The all-night Brasserie in the Fairmont was too expensive. The commuter eggeries on Lombard are just, oh, okay. The varicosed waitpersons are more fun than the omelets. So I found my way to the edge of the Tenderloin and Brother Juniper's Breadbox, Raphael House, the Holy Order of Mans — this is all one place. At first I thought it might be some sort of do-gooding resort for the down-and-out, wrong for my purposes. I'm only sometimes morally down-and-out at dawn, afflicted with memories and nostalgias; financially, I can pay my way to the appropriate proteins, carbohydrates, vitamin C, and caffeine. But Brother Juniper's, while inexpensive, is a genuine public breakfast resort, open at 7:00 AM, just in the nick of time when I hike down from Russian Hill.

If I'm a little early, I can lurk in the doorway with a legal secretary or two, a geezer, a fretful insomniac, an occasional German tourist family from the hotel next door.

For news of the food and service details, please see some other rubric. This is not a restaurant review. This is a review about hanging out alone as the sun comes up over SFO.

Brother Juniper's serves my purpose: tables large enough to spread a newspaper on, natural light for reading, unobtrusive baroque music, good ventilation, and the company of early risers similarly inclined: meter persons, seniors with paperbacks, sleepy couples ending a night to remember. Smiling in their blue clerical garb, the folks who serve the muffins and oatmeal, eggs and toast, look like young folks gone right. They may be ordained, for all I know, but their missionary position is: "How do you want those eggs?" There is no scent of fanaticism.

I've become a frequent flier at Brother Juniper's, and have learned a little about the other frequent fliers. There is a young woman with a stack of books by and about Virginia Woolf. She is preparing her dissertation on the Bloomsbury heroine in this holy lunchroom.

There is a wistful young man who has come from Hawaii to make a career in San Francisco as a professional essayist. Over the past year, I have occasionally traded newspapers with him, or overheard a snatch of his conversation, or learned a little about him in the normal familiar politenesses of morning: "Haven't been around lately, have you?" "Went home to Waikiki to see my mother." He has a sad, sad story: "It's not easy to make a living as a professional essayist in San Francisco."

He marks up and clips from the *Chronicle* and the *New York Times*, carefully studying every page, even the electronics goods advertisements. He likes to use a whole table as the headquarters for his small essay business, but doesn't mind sharing it with an occasional young male stranger, explaining about the diminished lot of a Montaigne or a Charles Lamb in the twentieth century. With young women, he generally remains silent, even dour, bearing the short-prose-form weight of the world — although once, I noticed he gave a friendly wink to an Oriental child and her mother.

The brothers and sisters who serve at Brother Juniper's Breadbox refer to each other as "Brother John" or "Sister Gloria," but there is no active conversionism going on here. It's muffinism, it's coffeeism. They run a professional operation. In season, tour buses wait outside and lines of English or German visitors come to stoke up before the visit to Muir Woods. I met a former masseur from the Press Club, now working as a tour guide. "Achtung! Achtung! Achtung! Pull down your tee shirts and let's get this show on the road!"

Sometimes, when the franc is right, French tourists gingerly approach the realities of American morning cuisine. I'm relieved to hear them call to each other in the too-loud voices of tourists everywhere — relieved because I'm an American and want other people, lost in strange climes, to have the usual Yankee flaws.

The neighborhood has a number of "residence clubs" catering to "seniors." I've watched one old man gradually carrying on more and more extended conversations with an invisible friend. But when the visible ones, like the Virginia Woolf scholar or me, wish him a good morning, he comes out of it, an alert and businesslike sparkle to his eye. He pounces on my newspaper when I leave it behind — sometimes even when I'm only going to the counter for a coffee refill. Alert synapses for the important coffeehouse-survival and save-twenty-five-cents matters.

I've admired a group of three, sometimes four young women, very attractive, who come in with dictating and computing equipment and set up in the corner along with their juice, coffee, and toast. The lawyer among them has hair that is just as nice as that of the secretaries.

I've watched many others and know nothing about them and enjoy their mystery. Usually, by the time I leave, the weather has changed — fog gone, sun up, the day about to begin.

No, the best part of the day is often over.

Fighting the Revolution
on Upper Grant

The mandolins make their funny windup plink-plink-plinking sounds and an innocent soul might think it's only a matter of music and enthusiasm at the regular weekend hard-string celebrations at the Caffè Trieste. A shrewd observer might detect a bit of flirtation here and there, a little footsie, a shared copy of *The New York Review of Books*, an occasional long, slow game under lowered eyelids. That stuff is obvious.

But beneath the happy Italian music, the excited hormones, and the reckless inhalation of caffeine fumes, there is also Maoism . . . old-fashioned Stalinism . . . the Course in Miracles and other radiant New Age guides to correct existence . . . even Werner Erhard's est, as defunct as Victoria Station steakhouses. Entire separate, obsolete revolutions are being plotted by the world-historical coffee drinkers at this traditional Bermuda Triangle, the corner of Grant, Columbus, and Broadway in North Beach.

Oh, assuming you are that shrewd but innocent observer, you may notice Dr. Jack Sarfatti, Ph.D., conducting his long-run seminar in advanced physics, medieval poetry, and the tragic love life of a contemporary genius.

You will also find Lawry Chickering, distinguished mover and shaper of the well-funded conservative thinkery, the Institute of Contemporary Studies, beaming and swaying to the folk rhythms of the band.

And there's Shig, who used to say he was an Eskimo, a retired manager of City Lights Bookshop, critic, publisher, grokker, and groover on the North Beach scene, stalwartly hanging out.

And there might be Henri Lenoir, former ballet dancer, former owner of Vesuvio's, the tavern whose slogan, "We are itching to get away from Portland, Oregon," inspired a generation. Art collector, repository of beatnik secrets, he works overtime at patrolling his beat, the permanent Mayor of North Beach.

These are some of the celebrities a visitor notices. They are ornaments of North Beach culture. They are tree shakers, jelly makers.

But now look in the corners, the dark and murky corners, in that dense maquis where certain folks hide behind barriers of fresh orange juice and caffè lattes. You may see only their sports sections, the statements of their trust funds, the bags of laundry that muffle their low and mysterious voices. In his madness, the great Nijinsky said: "People who think too much are martyrs." Nijinsky was a wise madman. These are the coffee martyrs of the Caffè Trieste. I'll conceal their real names here.

Over that wall near the Ladies and Gents is a diehard supporter of the Cultural Revolution in China. He seems not to remember that China later disavowed this brutal setback in its development. "The People came into the offices and discovered that officials had a Landlord Mentality," he says.

"How did they know?" I ask him. "How does a mob breaking into a building learn such a thing?"

"The People is never wrong," he states, sipping from a North Beach People's drink, cream soda.

I tell him about the visiting Chinese journalist I met, a well-educated editor, fluent in English and French. During the Cultural Revolution, he was sent to inoculate baby pigs on a pig farm. Does that seem appropriate employment for a trained editor? (As a writer, of course, I have wished this job upon many editors.)

"The People decided what he should do," said the North Beach Maoist. "He needed to go to the Countryside. He needed to be Reeducated."

On the terrace at Enrico's, the visiting Chinese editor had unbuttoned his shirt to show me the scars on his chest. "Baby pigs don't like to get their needle," he said. "Pigs bite, you know."

21

Said the North Beach Maoist: "Landlords bite their tenants."

And then there is the psychedelic Stalinist. He still believes in LSD; he still believes in the world revolution of the unified proletariat. Since he knows of my interest in Haiti, he brought me a petition to sign on behalf of the True & Faithful Communist Unity Party of Haiti. "I too am a lover of the Haitian workers and peasants," he said.

I studied the petition. It was in Spanish. The name of the Party was also given in Spanish. This puzzled me. "Haiti's language is French or Creole," I said.

"It is?"

"If you're a lover of Haiti, I'm sure you know that."

"But in South America, Spanish is the language of the Revolution."

This slowed me down. While waiting and keeping silent, I filled my silence with a few words: "Haiti isn't in South America. I guess you could say it's in Central America, sort of, that's close, but actually it's on a Caribbean island."

The leader of the Haitian workers and peasants cast a look at me that said: *Details, bourgeois details.*

And at a round table (round to celebrate the Eternal Gaia in us all) sits a true believer who has embraced one California faith after another, including est, the Course of Miracles, and now the First North Beach Fundamental Church of the Divine Bull Session (Post-Doctoral, Old Faith). I've slightly altered the name of the church in order to protect innocent California cults.

"I enjoy only cosmic art," he informed me.

"How can you tell what's cosmic?" I asked.

"I went to Berkeley."

"So?"

"So I know."

Although normally eager to accept the argument of Truth by Authority (it saves having to think), on this occasion I sought to shed more light upon the divine radiance of his Berkeley-trained mind. "Give me an example of cosmic art."

"Art that's . . . cosmic."

That should have satisfied any normal seeker. But I plunged on, feeling like a foreign correspondent in Coffeehouse Land. "An example, please. How about a cosmic novel?"

"Don't read many novels."

"A painting?"

"That's decoration. I prefer my own visions, man."

"Well, how about *anything* cosmic. Give me any example of cosmic art you choose."

He searched his inner softwear. He scanned the floppy disk. He came up with: "The songs of Andrew Lloyd Webber. Leonard Bernstein's *Candide.*"

"Tell me about Mr. Webber — is that with-one-*b* Weber or two-*b*'s Webber? Which songs?"

"I think he wrote *Evita.* I think he wrote, what's that hit on Broadway now, *The Ghost of the Opera.*"

"Phantom. *Phantom of the Opera.*"

His gaze upon me was triumphant. "You're learning," he said. "That was a test."

Since I had flunked his exam, I felt free to drop the

course. I joined a friend in another part of the crowd. She was swaying to the massed mandolin gang. On a Saturday morning, she was doing the right thing.

A few minutes later, the cosmic philosopher pushed his way through the assemblage. "Listen," he said, "I think we should talk about why we're not able to communicate."

I felt we were communicating adequately. The problem was what we were communicating. And clarification with Cosmic Man would also morally oblige me to clarification with the Stalinist and the Maoist. It would be only fair. And on a fine Saturday morning in North Beach, that would be more clarification than any of us needed. Quite properly, Sarfatti, Chickering, and Shig were devoting all their attention to the music.

The mandolin is an instrument that plays the same note again and again. And the mandolins played on.

Who Is the Reverend Ted McIlvenna, M.Div., Ph.D., and Why Is He Sowing These Wild Oats?

Before Shirley MacLaine opened up her profitable past-life guru franchise, she had interests more in keeping with her youthful personae: erotic art. Somehow, during those dear, dead days so frequently recalled — the San Francisco flower epoch — she got involved with an odd couple who traveled and published under the unique byline "the Drs. Kronhausen." He Doc was a small, slim fella with Nehru-suit-era bangs. She Doc was a large and enigmatic blond woman.

Together, with la MacLaine ardently promoting, and under the capable guiding hand of a cheerful San

Francisco scholar and Methodist minister, the Reverend Ted McIlvenna, they donated a generous collection of sexy stuff to the Museum of Erotic Art on Powell in Downtown Ess Eff. At the grand opening I stood eating sushi with the actress (and this was *really* a past life) in front of an Indian sex scroll depicting behaviors that Americans were only beginning to practice. As a matter of fact, we may not yet be as good at them as the almond-eyed Hindu athletes in the scroll. This was only the beginning of sushi-eating in America, too.

The Erotic Museum, which seemed to scream out over the cable car line, "Tax Scam! Tax Scam!" was nevertheless an appropriate decoration for the swinging San Francisco of that time. Eventually the city tore up the street, the tourists were derailed, and the Drs. Kronhausen took back their art. Some of it seems to have been damaged or lost in a mysterious sea accident. The good Drs. moved to Costa Rica. If the Indian sex scroll lies at the bottom of the ocean, perhaps it offers evening entertainment to the wild sushi swimming about in their eerie limbo.

The good part remains. Something has been prospering and thriving and diligently going about its task. The Methodist and Marshall Field–funded Institute for Advanced Study of Human Sexuality, the Reverend Ted McIlvenna, M.Div., Ph.D., prop., is enlarging its quarters down on Franklin Street. Ted has been in this business for years now; Ted is large, jolly, robust, vibrant, a living advertisement for the benefits of advanced study.

He supervises students and faculty. People come from all over. He consults; he advises. He has collected a library, books, tapes, films, documents; he has gathered objects both rare and common. There are curators and outreach programs, classes and inreach programs. There is even a kind of campus hangout — a Korean eatery down the block. His serious accumulation of toys, games, devices, souvenirs, battery-powered relics, and rubber or plastic equipment doesn't weigh down his spirit. I think it's metabolism that keeps him so happy, but maybe it's the good that he does. This is one heck of a lively Methodist we have here.

I renewed our acquaintance after years of following separate paths. You might be asking: How could someone *forget* about the world's center of sex research? (Never mind Kinsey in Indiana; small solemn potatoes.) Well, that's San Francisco, so many attractions, where the Institute for Advanced Study of Human Sexuality can just plumb slip a person's mind. But a magazine asked me to report on "the corporate call girls" — women who bring their traditional software to the male and female executives of Silicon Valley — and said that the Reverend Ted McIlvenna could offer the necessary information and insights, including the vital insight of a few telephone numbers.

He doesn't merely wish to increase knowledge and happiness. He is a scholar in all the folkways of the sex industry. He keeps helpful tabs. He's the man for me.

Besides, he has that Celtic enthusiasm, the appreciation of fun, that our modern world of today can use a bit more of. At least my part of it.

The institute had been torn up for extensive remodeling. It will soon have computerized television resources for programming, reprogramming, and deprogramming. They will be able to press a button and visions will float on the walls. When I dropped by, walls were down, boxes and sex litter were scattered everywhere. We kicked our way through obsolete rubber goods. Mystical paintings of jewel-encrusted activities, a reproach to folks of my staid temperament, were stacked in halls, awaiting pickup. There is so much to collect and so little storage space. There were crates containing the master molds from which the Popeye and Tillie the Toiler comic books, Tijuana versions, educated a generation of fine American boys who soon went off to war. Ted picked up a handful of pamphlets and said, "Here, keep these," and added, "Fella who published them is still in prison, last I heard."

The building was filled with interns, grad students, sex therapists, video experts, your average midday crowd in pursuit of learning. Motherly Mrs. Winnie McIlvenna, wife of Ted, sent us out to lunch without her — too darn much to do. At Kim's Korean Short Order — it's actually called the Elite, and Ted treated — we talked about one of the institute's new projects, Exsativa, Swiss Formula A111.

Here we go, down the hatch with Ponce de León. Exsativa is an alleged aphrodisiac produced by a natural substance drawn from green oats. No, not an aphrodisiac. A stimulant that conserves the hormonal energies of the body. So it's not a medicine, not a drug, but a magic food. Magic if you're interested, anyway.

The Institute for Advanced Study of Human Sexuality is interested, and probably so is everybody else. As Ted McIlvenna told the story, it all began with lazy-breeding Chinese carp who suddenly perked up and spawned like crazy when unripe oats were dumped into their cozy ponds. Remember the saying "Sowed his wild oats"? or: "Feeling his oats"?

Folk wisdom and popular speech seem to have been onto something, but they forgot to say *green.* The Chinese carp, who got the green oats, are not known to respond to placebos. The extract is made by a Swiss company under the name Exsativa, Swiss Formula A111. Tests are continuing, but there is already lots of anecdotal evidence in the research report, including human clinical trials, sponsored by the institute. (Account Executive, sixty-five: "Embarrassing but wonderful." Executive, forty-five: "She's happy, I'm happy, but will it last?" Insurance Executive, fifty-eight: "My wife . . . wants some.")

My favorite comment comes from Office Manager, forty-one, who reports great sexual restoration after a period of impotence but complains about the powder: "Can't you put the product in a pill? I don't drink tea and I hate juice."

Now there's an office manager who is hard to please.

About the foregoing: I'm only giving the facts as I know them. Don't call me; call the institute.

As we discussed Exsativa, I ate chicken salad. There was no green oatmeal on the menu. We were joined by a lovely graduate sexology student from Australia who moved over with her Cricket lighter and her crumpled pack of cigarettes. I often manage to do all the wrong things. Just when we were becoming good friends (Australia is a fine place, great beaches, terrific kangaroos), I said, "Now that you've got sex down pat, let's see if we can arrange a scholarship for you at Smokenders."

Ted beamed paternally. Later I apologized. Graciously, on the lovely Australian's behalf, he waved it off. In the sex study biz, needing to deal with foundations, the government, the courts, folks who tear up Powell, and folks who go off pouting with their Indian sex scrolls — plus some of the flaky people that come around — hail-fellow-well-gracious is the ticket. I want to say I admire this man, an endearing and enduring personality in our great metropolitan village, a Methodist minister like none other, a delectable mountain, to use e. e. cummings's phrase, surviving and thriving and teaching us how in the era of Safe Fun. It's not his job to stop the students from smoking.

Stop-Action on
Russian Hill

The little shop at the corner of Jones and Broadway was one of those traditional Italian family groceries — the hard stuff, like cereal and soap, plus a few bananas and tomatoes and cartons of milk in a dusty case. Some of these Russian Hill bananas were so mature, freckled, and brown that they showed signs of wanting to walk poodles and complain about the changes in the neighborhood. But the store served the locals, who could run out early in the morning or late in the evening and find what they needed or at least get advice on how to make do with canned applesauce instead of yogurt.

We know the stock turned over because sometimes we saw the family in their black Buick at the Safeway, loading up with apples. Then they raised the price to an appropriate convenience-store level. We didn't mind if the neighborhood grocer turned out to be a Safeway intermediation system. At his post on Russian Hill, Tony watched over things. With his arms crossed over his apron, he stood sentinel.

When I moved in nearly thirty years ago, Russian Hill was a quietness floating above the beatnik adventure of North Beach and Chinatown, and only on weekends could you occasionally hear the yelps and wa-hoos of tourists and the servicemen r&r'ing between tours of Vietnam. The squeak of mimeograph machines churning out beat poetry kept no one awake, nor did the sun-rustle of drying ducks on the rooftops of Chinatown.

Tony sold his shop to a Chinese man, or rather, to a Chinese family. Oddly enough, the new owner was also called Tony. The dusty milk-and-cheese case, the tomatoes, the bananas ripening toward crotchety intelligence — I heard one complaining it was no longer a banana but a still life — the stock of Kellogg's and Jell-O and soap showed the same good judgment about emergency-supply requirements. There was also wine and the mixes. I watched Tony Two's children grow into adolescence.

The most vivid moment of Tony Two's tenure came when I caught a kid trying to steal my car. I dragged him by the ear into the store and yelled, "Call the police," as the boy cried and cringed.

"Phone not for public use," said Tony.

"Call the police!"

Tony said softly, "Call his father."

I held the boy and let him telephone home. The father arrived a few minutes later, having received a message I didn't intend. He was waving a knife — waving it at me — and I tossed him his son. Evidently I was interfering with get-up-and-go in the new world. What I remember about Tony the Second's tenure was his little smile.

When Tony the Second left, the corner stood empty for a couple of years. We missed the quick news fix, tomato fix, Monterey-jack fix. With the bananas gone, I had to make new friends.

Then a lady with a German accent came with measuring tapes and decorators. She had an *East* German accent, someone said, as if this were significant. She intended to open a little Russian Hill café, both elegant and comfortable, where folks could have their breakfast coffee and muffin and read the newspapers amid baroque music before heading for work downtown or the day's serious loafing. Some of the neighbors believed this would bring a parking catastrophe, still more cars in a place already afflicted with automotive peristaltic anxiety. They objected to her restaurant permits.

Dressed in grandmotherly weeds, handkerchief around her hair, she canvassed the neighborhood with a petition. Wouldn't we enjoy a little European café on the corner? Croissants? Cappuccini? Fresh-squeezed orange juice?

Of course we would. I signed the petition. I didn't mind the East German accent if it brought baroque music, newspapers from elsewhere, bran muffins from Just Desserts.

Alas, it turned out not to be an adorable little café for hanging out, not at all. I had always wanted to use the word *adorable* in a positive way, but once again reality frustrated me. It was a chic and expensive little Russian Hill restaurant that would surely have complicated the parking problem except that it got bad notices from diners and critics. Few automobiles or people came. So the lady closed it, took down the sign, and then put up a different elegant sign and reopened her jewel box restaurant.

It didn't work. There was gloom in the little space where Tony One and Tony Two had thrived. It felt like Berlin during the blockade. Frau East Germany closed once again.

Next a Middle Eastern entrepreneur, along with a South American cook, opened an Italian restaurant. The proprietors were smiling and affable. The waitress, wife of the cook, was a new mother; and then, rolling her eyes, told me she was ready to have another child (not during my dinner, however). The place was inexpensive, attractive, unpretentious, and it was perishing. Not enough people wanted to take lunch or dinner on a quiet corner of Russian Hill inhabited by widows, former beatniks, a few artists and writers, remittance families, yuppies, and some stray millionaires levitating above the serious action of North Beach.

And thus appeared Angelo Quaranta. Angelo Quaranta rode out of the east. Angelo Quaranta charged up the hill, accompanied by Pamela Berman, a wistful and observant young woman. A bearded insurance man with a world-class Italian accent, Angelo described himself as "Beeg-Belly Cook." He liked food and wine. His laughter swept away the memory of food fumbles. "First, no more freezer," he announced. "All fish comes by telephone, fresh!" (I used to think it came by ship or airplane.) He called the new restaurant Allegro.

A sleepy outcropping of Russian Hill suddenly had an active center, with dinner guests like Art Agnos, mayor, and Richard Hongisto, supervisor, and the television actor who played Lou Grant — do I have to remember his name? — and gourmet visitors attracted by the rumor of fun. (Okay: *Ed Asner.*) Ed Moose and the Washington Square Bar & Restaurant were gracious enough to allow an extension of their media franchise. "This is an Italian restaurant?" people ask, and modest Angelo roars: "The only one in America!"

America has long needed an Italian restaurant. I thought there was one in Cleveland, my hometown, serving spaghetti and meatballs, and I hear that pizza can be found in New York — also, announcements and rumors of it, with promises of free soda, appear under my windshield wiper most mornings — but Allegro seems to be the authentic trattoria article. The jolly beeg-belly cook now stands triumphant under his tall white chef's hat where Tony the Sicilian, Tony the Chinese, the German disciplinarian, and the Middle Eastern entrepreneur sometimes stood and then passed into the valley of the shadow of forgetfulness. The nice thing about not having Alzheimer's disease is that you get to remember the past while living in the harmoniously garlicked present.

I still miss the bananas of the Tonys One and Two.

A Fable of
Montgomery Street

Call him Ishmael. When Lester Ishmael decided to have adventures and make his fortune, he didn't want to get his hands dirty. In fact, he didn't want to do too much work. These were the waning years of the twentieth century, this was Northern California, and he only wanted to enjoy his wife, treasure his daughter, and think deep thoughts.

What he preferred was to play some kind of game. Not Frisbee, not squash. He wished to have fun while getting rich and keeping his hands clean.

The stock market came to mind.

However, Ishmael didn't know how to crunch numbers. He didn't understand industries or science. What he had studied was Freud and the English language. He decided to play the market according to Freud and rhetorical clues. He would examine words and pay attention to what they revealed about the lusts of others. He didn't like to use Gordon Gekko's word, *greed*, because it failed to take into account all the laughs a clean-handed person might achieve on the winding road to millionairedom.

It turned out to be easy. That's a common beginning to a story of modern fortune-getting, and the story usually ends with a moral pang — the guy loses either his money or his soul. Hey, can't have both, fella. However, the rules have been altered in recent times, along with the wearing thin of the Me Decades and the threatened implosion of the Universe of Yup.

Clever Ishmael. Clever, clever Lester Ishmael. One evening while studying *Barron's* and the *Wall Street Journal* — on Mondays his wife went to her yoga class — Ishmael found just what he was looking for. He found a company hit by serious troubles, gone from 90 to below 30 on the New York Stock Exchange, whose CEO said: "Should we be found legally liable for the mistakes of our subsidiary, we would feel morally obliged to meet its obligations."

Beeps rang in Ishmael's head. That subjunctive and conditional "should," that weasel "would," that progression from "legally liable" to "morally obliged" — oh, no, they wouldn't pay. That confident unction in the phrasing by a CEO, MBA, rimless-glasses, CPA, LLD, devoted contributor to such good causes as an endowed professorship in Partly Owned Subsidiary Studies at Stanford Business School. They wouldn't pay. The market didn't know it yet, but they had found a way.

Ishmael bought the stock at 28. Sure enough, the company found a hole in the thicket of regulations. The price of the stock soared back toward 90 at the good news that moral obligation followed precisely from legal but in this case there was no legal. Ishmael made his first pile. He rejoiced. He took his wife to dinner at Ventana in Big Sur. (They spent the night.)

He wanted more piles.

He quit his job teaching English literature to business students at the University of San Francisco. He had tried to suggest that a knowledge of the smarm of Polonius, the evil grief of Richard III, the despairing shrewdness of Hamlet might help them thrive in the savings-and-loan business, but he convinced no one. Of course, he didn't understand what complicated schemes might be hatched by his students when they became loan executives, sitting behind Formica desks with the phones not ringing. Polonius, Richard III, and Hamlet didn't offer a whole lot when a person sought to make his fortune by supporting house remodeling enterprises in the Sunset and the Richmond.

But he did convince himself that the ambiguities and deviltries of grammar and psychology could be turned into successful stock ownership. Even into the successful sale of stock he didn't own. He expanded his field of operations.

Ishmael had a child in nursery school. He loved his wife, he loved his daughter, he loved his immersion in the recent world of Yup. He devoted three evenings a week, sometimes more, to the study of the financial press. His wife devoted three evenings a week, sometimes more, to the flexibility of her spine, the lion's roar, advanced yoga for total fulfillment. While Ishmael spent much of his time on his researches into Freud, literature, and the *Wall Street Journal*, he also took his wife to the restaurants they could now afford. He carpooled their daughter in the Honda Prelude — up from Civic, leapfrogging Accord — which they could now afford. Ishmael was raising his standing in life with methodical caution.

One doesn't choose the parents of one's four-year-old's nursery-school best friends. It happened that Ishmael met the president of a San Francisco company listed on the Pacific Exchange and found something a little shifty in his gaze. But shiftiness of eyes might be only a romantic image for shiftiness of character, and at any rate, he was only the father of another cute four-year-old in pigtails, thought Ishmael. He could be shifty to beat the band as long as he delivered the kids to school on time on his day.

But the man gave Ishmael his card, in the folkway of folks of a certain discipline, and there was his name printed in raised blue and white: JÉRÉ McGRAW.

Jéré?

"Jayray?" Ishmael asked. He had studied French.

The man blushed. "It's pronounced Jerry."

Ishmael meditated upon the character and reliability of a Jerry who spelled his name like Jayray. Gosh, he controlled all that money. Gosh, he must be a creep. Not only shifty but dumb enough to be caught.

Ishmael sold the stock short at 8. And sure enough, despite the boom days, the company hit Security-and-Exchange shoals, accounting whirlpools, fraud rocks; it foundered. Ishmael covered his stock at 0 — ¹⁄₁₆, to be exact. Ishmael's insight about a Jerry who transmogrified himself into a Jéré gave him his second pile.

Now Ishmael looked for a bar called Hubris in which to celebrate his skill, his wit, his insight, and his cheerful intelligence. Hubris, of course, is that Greek sin which leads a man to compare himself to the gods or the Boeskys. It was also the sin that totally bored his former students at USF. Ishmael ran a scan on his heart, but found none of this mad pride. All he discovered was a quiet satisfaction, plus love of his wife, his child, his life in San Francisco, plus maybe a little *amour-propre*.

Perhaps, he thought, the bar in which he might celebrate should not be called Hubris but Meritocracy. Hey, nice name for a Montgomery Street tavern.

Then one day he came home and his wife said to him: "You're happy —"

"I am. I am."

"You're happy, you like what you do, you're satisfied with your fate, you think you're in control."

"Yes, a little. And?"

"And I want someone who needs my help. You *don't*, buster. My yoga teacher has terrific problems, and you didn't even notice —"

"Pardon? How should I? I never see him."

"— and you don't even notice" — but indeed, he was beginning to notice — "you don't even notice I'm leaving, I'm going to go with someone who needs me, I'm finished with this phase in my life."

Lester Ishmael fell silent. His wife had given him something new to think about.

"However," she added kindly, appreciating his good nature and his lack of imagination, which was only now beginning to make him suffer, "you can visit our kid as much as you want. You know I'll not throw away the memories of you as a good daddy who sometimes carpooled the kid to nursery school for fun and profit."

Sea Tides at the
Neighborhood Café

Two big things qualify the coffeehouse as one of the great inventions of modern civilization. You can go to meet people on friendly neutral ground. And you can go to the friendly neutral ground *not* to meet anybody.

Is that only two things? Try a couple more. You can meet strangers. You can bask in the jolly noise and sights of strangers you don't meet.

In addition, you can read your paper, write your poems, fill your journal, compile your lists of things to do tomorrow. If the café is right, the light is right, the music or lack of music is right, the heat and energy and ventilation are right, you can also explore the comforting rightness of coffee and muffins. You might want to dream of jungles and wars in the coffeehouse, but it is more certain, when in a jungle or a war, you'll dream of the café.

I've traveled across continents from one language to another and in every city find one where I can converse in the international bohemia of café life. I'm not talking about boîtes, clubs, entertainment places. I'm talking about hangouts. "Hey man, what's happening?" is the pass phrase. When I leave San Francisco, I discover a little San Francisco elsewhere, and not just in Moscow, Paris, New York, Port-au-Prince, or Jerusalem. There's Arabica in Cleveland. There's Benjamin Two in Milwaukee. There's even a bit of Berkeley in Milwaukee and Cleveland.

San Francisco populations wash up on the shores of the neighborhood café, getting into coffee and the newspapers and the throwaways left behind by other passengers passing through their routines. At school I had a teacher who argued that cafés are responsible for the Industrial Revolution, for the change from peasant and feudal life into whatever we have now. Lloyd's of London was a coffeehouse; you can't have investment without insurance; you had insurance because people — mostly men in those days — could sit around pooling their bets on whether the ship might arrive. They made deals. They made arrangements.

Thanks to coffee, they didn't go to bed at sundown.

Alcohol keeps people up, too, but on alcohol you don't generally organize yourself or anything else. You tend to slop around; a few artists can function that way, but most creative folks do better on the oceanic, clear-headed high of strong brew. (Balzac died young, probably because he wrote the thirty-some volumes of *The Human Comedy* on a dose of forty cups a day.)

Coffeehouses instead of saloons means people talk, gossip, read, think, and organize not merely insurance cartels. Perhaps my old teacher is right. Civilization as we know it is based in the Café de Flore in Paris, the Blue Bird in Moscow, and Le Petit Café in San Francisco.

When I lived as a student in Paris, I inhabited a room without a shower, toilet, or heat. It was so small that when I tried to give myself a shower by splashing at my shivering body from the sink, my wife crouched under an umbrella in the opposite corner. Writing a first novel, I needed privacy and heat. The agitated and smoky anonymity of a coffeehouse provided a kind of enlightened privacy; bodies and espresso machines provided heat. I took on Left Bank bohemian habits *because they made sense.* I could look up from my notebook onto scenes of political warfare, amorous negotiation, business dealing, black market and criminal-brinky manipulations — vanity, fun and survival scenes — and then go back into my dream life. Gosh, this was existentialism, this was how to be an artist, this avoided the awful isolation of writing a book while offering all the marvelous isolation the career of book writer demands.

Now I do much the same in San Francisco — at Malvina's in North Beach, at Just Desserts in the Marina, at Brother Juniper's in the Tenderloin, and at Edible Delight and Le Petit Café near where I live on

Russian Hill. Like a bar band, I change locales so people don't get tired of my tunes. I keep my anonymity. I used to drink hot chocolate in Paris, trying to keep all that caffeine in the brain from ruining the prose with excess jazz; then alternating chocolate and coffee for the warmth. Chocolate coats the teeth; I don't want to be a coffee junkie; I've moved toward decaf and grapefruit juice. In San Francisco, the dark-roasted decaf and the fresh-squoze juice, rushed to the table before it spoils, are a definite improvement over Paris products. That's why San Francisco is more important in the arts than Paris these days. As we will all agree.

Grace Paley, when she used to sit in Washington Square Park with her children, explained what she was doing: "I have to raise my kiddies. And also, since that takes fifteen or so years, I'm studying the sociology of the Square."

Since I have to write my books, I've also learned something of the sociology of the cafés. Take Le Petit Café, for example. It opens at 7:30 AM to a rush of financial-district yuppies and a few workmen in jeans. There are briefcases, running shoes, *Wall Street Journal*s, *Chronicle*s, and the *New York Times* doing the steamed eggs, plates of fruit, refills and refills of coffee. Perhaps ten percent of the early morning crowd is coupled — the married ones with shared newspapers, the afterglow ones with shared glances, bumps, and touchings, and also newspapers (this is a weekday morning, after all). A little later come the young parents with kids, needing to get out of the house or getting the tyke to child care. Then come the layabouts, the ones doing their horoscopes, dealing the tarot cards; they are mixed with the power-breakfast conferees and those like me who settle in to do some heavy thinking and light ingesting or light thinking and heavy ingesting. As the morning wears on, you find regulars finishing their aerobic runs with a bran muffin and something in a cup or glass. The double-parked cars are a mix of sporty items, serious jalopies, and practical Hondas. Le Petit Café does its share to cure the city's budget deficit. Meter folks plant a lot of windshield wipers with red-zone, fire-hydrant, and double-parking citations.

As lunchtime approaches, the long-term renters of tables make room for salad eaters. A few students from the Art Institute. Light lunchtime pickups. Some of those in running sweats are only doing their laundry at the launderette next door.

Tourists come in carrying their guidebooks for comfort. "Hey, look, books for sale in a coffeehouse!" (There is also a continuous exhibit of paintings, prints, and photographs by local artists.) I enjoy the sight of those with perfect lip gloss and eye shadow to match their Esprit laundry-doing clothes. I enjoy those with spreadsheets and reports, the ones who push tables together for meetings. "Okay, let's conceptualize the project, I got a few figures here." I feel more empathy with the single residents, sometimes mumbling to themselves, of whom I am one. But hey, I'm not against networking or group conceptualizing. Existentialism is a church with many cathedrals, some with second mortgages.

Once, a frequent coffee drinker had her nervous breakdown at Le Petit Café. She was an Iranian immigrant and she was sobbing and laughing and apologizing for the disturbance. When her family came to get her, an uncle shook hands with each of us before they led her away. "I hope she did not interrupt your studies, sir," he said to me.

My mother in Cleveland had often warned me that coffee makes people crazy.

Late in the afternoon the yuppies, the young parents with kids, and the nondrinking hillside strollers return to say good-bye to the day before beginning the serious work of evening. The waitpersons light candles and set out linen napkins. The coffeehouse becomes a restaurant and that's another story. I won't tell it, because I spend more of my evenings at the Puccini on Columbus, where the music is Italian popular or Puccini arias, the population is North Beach Italian and Beatnik Survivor, and the light is good for reading.

Existentialism lives! The Industrial Revolution is home free in San Francisco coffeehouses.

A Couple of
Monogamous Lovers

"**T**hese days monogamy is important," she said.

"But is it possible?" he asked with genuine curiosity.

"Everybody's gradually aiming that way, Brian —"

"A little bit at a time?"

She realized this was a hard case — a veteran extra man, a Brian who obeyed all the stop signs in Pacific Heights, a frequent escort of those bereaved after seven-year marriages, a person who could fit himself into the business trips of young career women, a San Francisco philosopher devoted to exploring the New Age. He recognized that Windham Hill wasn't Mozart, but argued that in Mozart's day, Mozart wasn't Bach. He didn't care if it made other people's kind of sense. He was onto himself, secure in his own nature.

People tended to like a man who so frankly and honestly approved of his own every move. They forgave him a lot. While forgiving him temporarily, Kimmie also tried to improve him.

"But if not a stable one-on-one, do you want to get It?" she asked. Getting *It* used to refer, during the good old days of est, to being in touch with the essential reality of how things were all focused on accepting yourself. Getting *It* now looked, with the hindsight of history, pretty good. These days It referred to AIDS. "Not to speak of herpes," she murmured seductively.

"Maybe you save old copies of *Time* and *Newsweek*," he said. "Herpes was a couple years ago's problem."

"You're being funny. If you've got it, it's not a couple years ago's. It's right now."

"I hear the itch wears off," he said.

"Well," she said, feeling she had him at her mercy at last — or at least she was making progress — "AIDS doesn't."

"I'm monogamous." He smiled with the shifty confidence of a man with an income, which was good, and also his own burden of troubles — couldn't touch the principal until he was forty, which was bad. "I'm monogamous with only a few people, one at a time." He realized smart talk could turn him into a loser here except at the game of smart talk, which was not the game he was interested in playing with this young woman at the present time. He was interested in touching the principal. "Hey, Kimmie, only kidding," he said.

She had a shag of chopped-off dark hair, a ferocious little French face, and he liked gamines. At this moment in history — five o'clock on a June Sunday afternoon, after tennis and a shower — he definitely liked gamines. "I really want to get monogamous with you, kid," he said.

She was a few years older than he was. She didn't like to be called kid. With her treatments, especially the eye job that did it for the smile lines, smoothing them into insignificance — and also now use the monster-strength sun block, please — she didn't look much older than the boy. The thirty-seven-year-old boy. But still: *not to call her kid.* This was too lovely a June after-noon after tennis and a warm shower together to lay all the cards on the table, but still. "I'm not your kid," she said.

"I don't have any other," he pointed out. "Never made that mistake of making a bad marriage or two. You're the one with the children."

"I call them babies."

He patted the banquette against which both of them were leaning. "Well, when they're old enough, maybe you'll call them kids. We don't know that yet. Why don't we wait and see before we reproach me for my oral lan-guage when we like my body language, hey?"

She hated quarrels. She especially hated quarreling in a nice, quiet hotel bar with soft music playing behind the plans people were making. The only people not making plans for the evening were a few businessmen, quieting themselves down with a drink or two before bed, hoping against hope that some better plan might present herself.

She knew that quarreling over irrelevant topics, which was what they were heading toward, was more revealing than the ones a person decided upon. Irrelevant topics erupted, they were dangerous, they made trouble. Her therapy had taught her this.

Trouble was, his therapy had taught him nothing because it was yet to come. So far, all his systems were up and go, and silly boy, he was looking forward to turning forty in due course. Then he could take control. And by that time, of course, when he could inform the trust account folks to go fuck themselves, she would be forgotten and some little chickie who was probably now in middle school would reap the benefit.

This was definitely unfair.

"Monogamate," she said, "did you invent that word?"

He smiled. "You did. You just did. I never even *thought* that word. It's not a thing I do."

He was a beautiful child. He was a beautiful but dumb child. What was she doing here with him? she wondered, and said, "How would you like to take me home now?"

"How I would like it is a whole lot."

"Are you going to do it?"

"I'm thinking. That's part of the whole foreplay deal."

He gazed with his sparkly-toothed smile into her face, putting his narrow-skulled head close to hers, his tanned skin showing little white lines from the smile that said youth and sun and health and tennis in a man — those same lines that a woman had to fend off with sunscreen, abrade away. Not fair, was it?

"You think too much," she said.

"I think too long maybe. But I don't think too much.

I'm just a little slow. I'm thinking: Aren't you a little afraid of me?"

Now she was on home ground. Fear was what she used to inspire in men. She understood it well. But there was nothing to fear from a man who wore a cotton tennis sweater under his blazer while chatting in a bar of the Claremont Hotel after tennis and a shower. He had no real doubts, but he still seemed to be considering taking her to bed. The only possible loss would come if she expected something of this man, but he was nothing; nothing comes of nothing; only something to do in the evening could come of this nothing. She had cried all her tears over other men.

The waiter stood by the table. Their glasses were empty. Hotel bars didn't change, only the decor sometimes.

The man waiting for her to decide, the man in the cotton tennis sweater, had a narrow, sinewy lap. It didn't bunch up like the lap of older, thicker men. Perhaps it was because of the attention he paid to his tailoring.

Patient and silent, he was still waiting.

Had it come to this for her?

It had come to this.

The Self-Packagers

Once upon a time there was a man who never shoplifted anything from his local Walgreen's or Safeway. This miracle extended back unto his seventh year. It's possible. It's not likely.

Once upon a time there was a woman who bench-pressed weights at the Bay Club like an Olympic champion and never took steroids. Not likely, but it's possible.

We won't worry about these occasional and self-protecting storymakers. They are ordinary folks like you and me, putting the best face they can imagine on things. Their skin got tight all at once because of . . .

because of . . . well, a lettuce diet and meditation. And that scar behind the ears is a hereditary fold that appears at age forty.

Big cities attract big liars — lifestyle liars, who invent themselves out of whole but sometimes dissolving cloth. The grand metropolitan village of San Francisco qualifies as a big city. These people, the lifestyle liars, should be called something kinder, gentler, in the manner of contemporary Bushismo — perhaps self-packagers.

"Hey man," said Max Magnus — not his real name — from his customary station at a window table at the Washington Square Bar & Restaurant. "I hear you're a writer and I'd like to make a movie out of one of your books."

"Which one?"

"You tell me, man."

A normally competent human being would recognize con and shuck, but writers are not normally competent. Wellsprings of hope gush eternally from their hyperventilating breasts. "You mean you haven't read the book you want to make a movie from?"

"Hey, I'm a busy mogul, just happen to have a lot going for me right now. Here —" And he thrust his card into my hand. Sure enough, proof positive, this guy must be on the up-and-up. MAX MAGNUS, PRODUCER-DIRECTOR. "So you just pass me a script — no paperbacks, please — and my people'll get back to you."

Do I take a meeting? I thought. Lunch?

I was standing with a glass of unfrozen orange juice at a Christmas cocktail party on Jackson in Pacific

Heights and I was having a good time. Contrary to the accepted judgment about such events, I felt full of peace, goodwill, admiration for the folks surrounding me in their sparkles and finery, pleasure in their company. Contrary to what people say about parties, I was glad to be invited. This can happen.

Juniper was pitching a little proposal at me. After all, this was the season to begin anew — why not begin anew *rich?*

"What exactly is it you do?" I asked.

"Start-ups," she said. "Take great ideas public."

In my college days, this would have meant Aristotle, Plato, Descartes, Spinoza. In more recent times, it means Apple, Gap, George Bush.

"Usually," I said, "as a bachelor, divorced, straight" — let's get out the basic data — "I make this kind of stand-up food work for dinner. I try to balance the walk-around shrimp with the pick-it-yourself carrot sticks. But how about we have dinner afterwards?"

"Better just keep our cars parked and we walk down to Just Desserts," she said. "It's downhill both ways, how I figure. Lots of decaf is what I need."

She was tapering off, she explained, from lots of caff, the hard stuff. Even without arterial stimulation, she was a take-charge financial planner. She also liked stand-up dinners — "grazing's more time-efficient than dining." Juniper's name suggested sweet-smelling fields and copses. Juniper's actual presence suggested that she left the city only for flying visits to the Golden Door.

Juniper, one of the great packagers, is a handsome young Stanford MBA who was currently running with her own software company. The first software she needed to produce or evoke or chase out of the woods was the money. Over decaf at Just Desserts, she was not shy about asking. "A share of letter stock," she said, "and legally you have to read the prospectus first — hey, the red herring — will probably go public, ten for one, in two years at a kind of profit I can't ethically project. I could do it, but securities law limits my words. Let me just hint I'm putting my brother and my mother into this deal."

"It's only a few people —"

"My favorite brother. My only mother."

"— only a few people can do what you're doing, Juniper."

"That way nobody steps on my toes. No one fights with me for the cab. No grabby lawyer gets to say they're just as unique as I am."

And she's modest, besides. Her ankles are a little thick, but she knows enough to wear pants suits. The rest of her bones are neat. Sharp jawline. Perfect grooming. She uses what she has and what God gave her — in this case, a Christmas party at which she didn't even have to hand her card around.

At a different level of economic striving, there's the poet I met at City Lights, downstairs, where the living is easy but the breathing is hard. It's musty down there among the wall graffiti left over from when these literary premises housed a fundamentalist church. (O Ye of Few Iambs, Repent!) We struck up a conversation about the meeting of Trotskyite revolutionary pamphlets and language poetry from Bolinas. "I've got," she said, "a poem coming out in . . ."

"Pardon?"

She had lowered her voice. "People are so jealous around here. Poets are the worst. *The New Yorker.*"

I uttered words along the line of hey, that's terrific, let's go over to the Tosca and listen to Jeanette Ethredge complain about the thumping noises from the disco downstairs. "It's a great bar, that leather, that friendly Jeanette, opera on the jukebox, all those ballet and movie people, and now you can be the real *New Yorker* poet."

"Hush," she said. "All I need is the jealousy to spread."

Dana was a graduate student at San Francisco State. Of course I knew she didn't have a poem coming out in *The New Yorker.* But I thought: Let us encourage, let us drink cappuccino, let us ride with the fibbing flow.

When I came to live in San Francisco thirty years ago, carrying all my baggage in one blue army barracks bag, it was still the time of people making themselves natives even if they weren't, heading out to the west and calling themselves Slim or Tex or Lucky and defining their history any damn way they pleased. The hustle of the sixties was a different hustle from that of the eighties, but it was still hustle. Folks hunkered down, looked for company, and didn't shuttle back east by jet so often. California was a different country. San Francisco was the city where nobody came first. We had all started on equal terms. A few sprinkles of Spreckels only confirmed the general consensus: no landed aristocracy, unless you wanted to count Ishi. It was expected that you might even turn out to be whatever you said you were — hoped and dreamed you were.

By the way, I exaggerated a little up there. It was only twenty-nine years ago that I arrived, and I had two blue barracks bags. See what I mean.

Now about Dana, that eager young poet whose approach to a stranger in the basement of City Lights was: Hey, my poem is coming out in *The New Yorker.*

Her poem came out in *The New Yorker.*

The Stanford MBA, Juniper, now works for another Stanford MBA, automating legal offices, and has temporarily gone back to drinking caff. She has a new start-up in mind. This one will definitely work.

In the city of eight hundred thousand stories, not counting South City or Marin, some of the stories turn out to be true. Max Magnus is a real director-producer of films. But they have titles like *Laura Loops the Loop* and *Miss Viva Comes to Play.*

At a deeper, deeper, *deeper* level, some of the true stories turn out to be untrue, also.

Perestroika
in Pacific Heights

The dinner showed glints of silver, candlelight, fine caviar with its black sparkling, this year's high-fashion vegetables, cautious fellowship, renewed *glasnost*. But after the brandy — more glinting in the air, this time with snifters in addition to cutlery — the hostess initiated a discussion of serious matters with the visiting Soviet diplomats.

Why don't they have the kind of freedom she enjoys?

Many Americans don't have it either, one of the goodwill visitors commented, looking about this magnificent house, product of five generations of San Francisco success, compounded semiannually.

But those who are capable, the hostess pointed out, rise in the world.

Those who choose their parents carefully, muttered one of the American guests.

"No one stops anyone!" cried the hostess, shooting a patriotic hate look at the disloyal travel consultant.

One of the Soviet visitors, the security official appointed to watch over the other diplomats, patiently pointed out what had stopped the USSR so far from equaling or surpassing the USA in consumer freedoms and products: "Great Patriotic War kill millions of Soviet citizen and infrastructure. Only now, thanks to frankly fine leadership, is recovery complete. Blu-jinzh now produced equal your San Francisco Levi production, plus automobiles up to level of Fiat with Italian technology, plus editions of classic books for all!"

The hostess looked puzzled. Personally, she preferred Japanese motor vehicles and French jeans. And nobody stopped her from buying them.

The KGB man shrugged. "Black market very popular in my country, too. Such as old ways of church."

The evening had reached the point where the Soviet delegation was seeking to conquer its drowsiness with cognac. This was the comfortable way to deal with jet lag, another Western disease that had spread to the Soviet Union in recent years, thanks to foreign travel. The leader of the group, the KGB man — described as a prominent critic and intellectual in the US-Canada Institute for Historical Analysis — waited for his glass to be filled so that he could offer a toast to *glasnost, perestroika,* rectification of racial injustice in US big cities, and increased fraternal exchange of computer technology. He held up the snifter and twirled it a little between his potato fingers, although nothing remained in the snifter to twirl except a little reflection from a face filled with longing.

Ever alert to the desires of guests, the hostess snapped her finger at the butler. She understood about hospitality and the details of good presentation of America for foreign visitors, having often been called upon by the State Department hospitality office in San Francisco. "Please!" she democratically ordered. "May we fill all the glasses one more time?"

There was an alert and respectful silence. The butler moved from place to place. There even seemed to be a bit of suspense and fear in the air, as if someone might be left out, although this had never before happened in history. The tension was dissolved by the butler's completing his round of the table.

The KGB man, a graduate in Suave, Doctor of Smooth, raised his glass. "To no more disagreements between Great Powers! To beautiful and generous hostess whom I invite to visit dacha in Peredelkino at her first opportunity! And above all — to Peace!"

The face of the hostess had compressed into a small and worried knot. Something he had said, or perhaps a level of brandy, which touched her heart, was causing inner turmoil. Normally she expected visitors from eastern Europe to be converted to the American way of life by dinner at her house. Generally the truth revealed itself to born-again totalitarians who pledged their allegiance in gourmet ceremonies. Indeed, in the recent past, certain Hungarian and Czech cultural leaders and designated hitters had finally confessed that the Soviet

61

occupation failed to regenerate all aspects of their lives. Even an East German filmmaker winked at her, a democratic gesture, although he also cupped his hand firmly and tightly on the back of her skirt when she stood by his chair to offer him a cigar.

After everyone drank, she rose and said, "May I ask only one more thing? That you give up converting others to your Communist way of life?"

The visitors shrugged. None chose to take the initiative.

Emboldened, she continued: "Hasn't history proven that you were wrong to try to export revolution?"

"Dear madame," said the KGB man, smiling, "there will remain points of frank discussion, the religious question, for example, or Africa, the Middle East, or control of the means of production, or several other matters on which a separate path by two great powers may be appropriate —"

"Do you mean —?" she began. But she had trouble phrasing the question. She had trouble understanding what he meant. She had trouble, at this point in the evening, understanding what she herself intended. She groped for a resolution to human and political dilemmas. Her eye fell on the butler. She summoned him with a nod. She whispered into his ear.

The Soviet visitors waited. Evidently she was preparing a little surprise for them.

The butler whispered back. He was not sure what she had in mind.

"Yes," she said aloud. "Exactly that."

The butler inclined his head at the English-butler-school obedience angle and walked up the winding stairway. The hostess watched and waited. The Soviet visitors glanced at each other. This was the kind of expectation that made conversation difficult, although a Soviet art critic managed to utter the words: "Asparagus at this season, very respectable agricultural achievement. But what exactly *is* asparagus?"

"A form of grass, only tastier," explained one of the American guests.

Now the butler, accompanied by a nurse, was moving slowly from the upstairs landing back to the stairway. What was this? They were leading two small children in all-cotton sleepwear. The children's paws were covered by embroidery. They stumbled and bumped against each other. They rubbed their eyes. They had been awakened and the little girl was whimpering at the command to come downstairs out of the middle of sleep.

Now the hostess was standing again. She commanded everyone's attention to the procession, butler, nurse, little boy, little girl. But all attention was there anyway, without her imperious gesture with her cognac snifter, which had somehow been filled during the summoning of her heirs.

"Look at them!" she cried. "These are my kiddies! And I adore them with all my heart! So do you," she said, directing the accusation at the KGB man, spokesman for the group, surely the authority who could answer for all of them, "do you really want to take these beautiful angels and make them into *Commies*?"

The Guardian Angels
Come to Camelot

In a time of heat and humidity, the strong oxidation of uncollected people makes the Tenderloin combat zone smell like Hell's Kitchen in Manhattan. No, said Matt Montes, local commander of the Guardian Angels, I wouldn't get to wear the red beret although I was spending Friday evening on patrol.

Identified mainly with New York, and with full frontal macho righteousness displayed mainly by young men, the national ten-year-old organization also includes women and an eighty-year-old. Curtis Sliwa, Founder, is now just thirty-five; his wife, Lisa, National

Director, fashion model, writer of a book on self-defense for women, was acting in a film being shot in Oakland while her colleagues hit some of the crack streets of San Francisco in their warning reds, tee shirts and berets, "daring to care."

In the Camelot Hotel, a welfare desolation row, filled with addicts, welfare cases, and lowest-level hustlers, I sat drinking coffee with a couple of Angels before hitting the streets. There was no combat equipment in this headquarters. A half dozen serioso young folks burdened with "no serious criminal records" (from the by-laws) prepared for their tours of duty.

The room on the third floor of the Camelot looked like something between an army dayroom, a police action room, and a boy's locker room — pots of basic beans and soup, tee shirts and telephones, walkie-talkies, filing cases half-open, a boom box, a blackboard with arrests listed, a wall with pinned photographs of crimes in progress and Angels making their citizen's arrests. There were some missing-child sketches. When an overweight trainee entered, fresh from working out at martial-arts drill in the basement — that is, unfresh from the exercise — someone said, "Man, I hope you're not gonna eat another twelve bags of chips before you go out."

Greg Mills was on the floor, looking under a desk. "I definitely smell a dead mouse," he said.

The names of the San Francisco Guardian Angels suggest one of the strengths of the group: Montes, DelRosario, Nguyen, Mounpak, Mills, Tom, Armstrong. One of the trainees I spoke with is half Italian, half American Indian, and raised in the Tenderloin.

This is nonvigilante group action by the people affected by crime. There is a fine line between fanatic vigilantism and citizen discipline. It was this fine line we walked on my nights strolling with them.

Greg Mills, leader of the patrol on my first visit, is a black ex-Marine, veteran of eight years of service, with intelligence training, fluent in Spanish, who once served as a guard at the US Embassy in Managua. He's done some reading and writing about Latin America and no longer supports US policy in Nicaragua. A tall, deep-voiced man, he looks like a young Sidney Poitier. He carried the walkie-talkie and brought a group of six Angels down Turk, up Ellis, across and back to Market Street, through the normal TL sidewalk population of hookers, transvestites, druggies, old folks, Asian kids, derailed tourists. He stopped to ask a sandy-haired, emaciated scarecrow who had been sitting on a street corner for hours: "You okay, man?"

The scarecrow was sober, not mumbling, and responsive. "Just sad," he said.

"You need something?"

"Just sitting here."

Greg waited a moment, and then we went on. The group was confronted by a thick, shaven-headed sport dragging along an empty-eyed obese girl with orange hair. The sport cornered one of the smallest Angels and shouted: "You get off my case!"

The young Angel didn't back away. It turned out he had interrupted a mugging four days ago; the sport had just gotten out of jail. During their conversation, the other Angels gathered in a little circle, their hands at the ready. It was head-to-head, and then suddenly the sport

broke off and swaggered down Ellis with the lady wad-
dling after him.

Greg was shaking his head and chuckling. "He got a
bad attitude," he said. "I talk to him, but he's *bad*. We'll
get him again."

A very tall man, even taller than Greg, danced up to
complain about being hassled a few nights ago by
Guardian Angels. "I had my little girl with me! That ain't
right, homeboy! Me and my lady was just rolling a joint,
going off to have a good time —"

Greg agreed and agreed; he shouldn't have been hassled if he wasn't threatening anyone; his child was with
him; maybe he was just in the wrong place to be rolling
a joint — agreed, agreed, agreed. It ended with a big
handslapping between homeboys, okay? And Greg said
to me: "He got mixed feelings about us."

There are moral ambiguities in the meeting of the
Guardian Angels and the Tenderloin, the TL, which
does not stand for Tender Loving. Most of the bad ones
on these mean streets are mere losers, like the girls
with dead eyes being run by pimps with darting eyes.
Maybe when they get their reward in crack or speed or
heroin, they liven up briefly. The Angels are using mus-
cle to protect the infirm; they sweep the garbage from
the streets. The garbage keeps raining down, like the
bottle that splashed on the curb near where we stood at
midnight. Perhaps the only people without moral am-
biguity are the children who stare from the storefronts
or hurry down Turk past the screaming, six-foot-high,
tottering transvestites. And some of the children are
running product for their mothers.

Street-smart do-gooders and do-strongers in an

American tradition, the Guardian Angels wear their red and white colors like a gang. They scrub the urban sink like missionaries. I've met likable Hell's Angels, too, so personal sweetness is not what supports the point. It's the ten years of steady persistence that begins to convince. The CIA is said to have "assets in place" for dirty tricks in foreign climes. The assets in place for the Guardian Angels are the people they encourage and organize in the Camelot Hotel, which is about as foreign as climes get, where the air is dusty with tiny bits of cash that people are trying to inhale in minor performance of major vices — hustling bodies, souls, and consciences.

A basic notion of neighborhood protection is to inspire the victims to fight back. By contagion, the local population discovers it can chase the bringers of plague. At the Camelot — a name that ironically evokes that teary fantasy of the Kennedy reign — the management welcomed the Guardian Angels. Since we remember the wasted hopes spent on guru-led organizations like Synanon and the Black Panthers, both of which rapidly degenerated, I looked for signs of megalomania. (Even the Hell's Angels were romanticized by flower-era softheads, served as bodyguards at Altamont.)

I visited the room of Caesar Cruz, formerly homeless, now an ardent catalyst for Camelot tenants. He kept his door open, feeling safe. The room was a friendly litter of phone, clothes, tables, papers, and a battered old portable typewriter. "I'm a writer, too," he said. "And I like to talk about what's happening here in the Camelot and on Turk Street. I'll be here, you want to talk."

There was still a dealer in the Camelot. All the

Angels could do was to wait, catch him, put the heat on, move him along.

"We're not going to end crime down here," Matt Montes said.

"Just be here and shine our flashlights in the corners," Greg Mills said.

We interrupted a group, two men and a woman, about to light up in a parking lot. They scurried. The Angels looked for glass litter. No grounds for a citizen's arrest, but the presence of the red berets makes the addicts uncomfortable. As we strolled, we got thanks from old people, women, and street folks who weren't necessarily harmless in other moods.

Everyone on the street seemed to use some sort of straightener or crookeder or placer-in-place that brought out the natural luster. When I asked Greg why the drinkers keep their bottles and cans in paper bags, the Gallo gift wrap, he said, "Custom. It's polite. Even if they're drinking soda pop." People express their natural luster any way they find available.

The natural luster of choice these days is crack cocaine, which makes for a rapid, purposeful walk, energetic gestures, imperative conversation with no necessity to have anyone to converse with. If there is opposition, or imagined opposition, conflict erupts. If the crack addict wants money, he wants it right now, with no opposition — violence erupts. These explosions of head bashings, auto bashings, knifings, shootings tend to concentrate the minds of everyone in the Tenderloin.

A small, skinny black girl, braces on her teeth, kept wanting to hug the Guardian Angels — even me, since I was along. Greg Mills called her Munchkin. She is a high-energy, pretty, very thin, happy-faced child who looks about fifteen years old. She *loves* the Angels. "How do you live?" I asked her.

"I live right here, on this corner." Pause. "Use to sell crack, but then I went to jail, so now I stopped. I hate that jail, man." Pause. During this pause she did not say how she lives now.

We met the Condom Lady, a young woman with her free wares lining her hatband, and she was greeted with enthusiasm, like a bunch of schoolkids getting their cocoa and graham crackers. "How many?" she asked, and if someone asked for a bragging lot, people said, "Whoeeee."

It occurred to me that the Tenderloin is as foreign a clime as Port-au-Prince.

Sitting with Supervisor Richard Hongisto, I listened to a cop complain that the Guardian Angels make trouble; they increase police work; they're not licensed. Hongisto said they make work because they call the police when they find trouble. Walking with the Angels one night, I saw cops wave from their passing cars, and when a huge thug confronted Ricardo, a Filipino Angel, sticking his finger in his face, begging for a fight, a police car pulled up and two cops leaped out, clubs raised. They massaged the thug in the belly, across the shoulders, and he took off running, nearly knocking down a hooker who was carrying a white flower. "He broke my flower," she wailed.

When the Angel patrol leader thanked the cops, one said, "We already had a call on him."

I asked Ricardo, who works as a cook in a restaurant in Oakland, if he was scared. "You *got* to be scared," he said. "You just can't let your fear overcome the rest of it."

A young man in a workout suit had jumped a closed fence to shoot a few baskets in Boedekker Park. "Hey man! Great!" he called, and Greg said, "You want to join us? Come by and take the training."

"I'll be there," the basketball player said, "I'll be there, man."

He might or he might not.

"We need everybody we can get," Greg said.

There's no money in this. It's almost un-American to see these people, a San Francisco rainbow of ethnicities and colors, spending their time as Guardian Angels when they could be hustling in the approved fashions. I asked Greg Mills, who is obviously a gifted young man, why he's here. "I'm an addictive personality," he said, laughing, "and I got involved, and now I'm hooked."

"You're from New York, Aren't You?"

On a misty winter-morning stroll down Telegraph Hill toward the moral encouragement of a cappuccino at Malvina's, I heard the hiss of hoses and the bullhorn of a chief before I saw the fire engines. The fire was out now. Water streamed down the slope. A wooden apartment house stood with its roof open to the sky and jagged rips where axes had been applied. It was like a shipwreck. There were blackened streaks down the wall. The smell of wetted ash was sharp and unpleasant.

A man I recognized from the streets of North Beach

stood watching against the fire department tape until a slicker-clad fireman chased him off. "It was my flat," he said to me. "Everything's gone, especially my art-work —" He didn't say paintings or sculpture; he said "artwork." "That bastard wanted to condomize the joint and we fought him, but you know how they are from New York. So he burned us out."

"Who?"

"Nat Grunes, you must know him, you're from New York, too."

I didn't know Nat Grunes from New York. "That's terrible," I said. "Do you have some friend where you can stay? I don't know him and I'm not from New York."

"The insurance, capische? That's why he did it. The insurance, and then he condomizes the hell out of us. Hey, you above all can figure it out."

I continued down the hill for my cappuccino, but the comfort of it was gone. I felt sorry for the artwork artist. I felt anxious because I was somehow accused.

The artist was waiting for me the next day, too. "Hey, you know how much Grunes is going to make on this deal? He condoms it and whammo, he's a rich little feller from Brooklyn or New York."

"The fire department has an arson department. Why don't you talk to them?"

"*You* talk to them. You know how they're in cahoots? One little guy brings the money, the other guy brings the certificate. The fix, man, just like they do in your hometown."

He hadn't shaved. He hadn't changed his clothes. I

didn't know where he slept. He was a tall, wracked man with eaten cheeks and a lurking, bothering manner. "Listen to this story you pretty much know already, man —"

"Right, right, but I'm on my way someplace."

As the days passed, I would peek at him from the corner before he saw me. He didn't stop other people. He watched the rotting hulk of his house in silence, breathing that ashy musk, that wet, swollen smell of water, ash, and rot. But then when he saw me, it started again. He ran after me. "You could set me up with a little money for a studio, give me a few good leads, your contacts and all, I'd gladly stop yakking at you like this. Must be aggravating, hey?"

"You've had a shock," I said.

"People in New York talk all the time on the streets, don't they? So you're used to it, those people like they got there in New York."

"Isn't there some provision to get you housing until you find a permanent —?"

"Hey, you know what kind of welfare state we got in the country? It's welfare for the arson landlords who want to condomize the place, that's what we got. It's welfare for the operators, man."

"You need to start working again," I said.

"Try. Just try. When they burn it out from under you so they can make a mint and go live back there, live big with some chickie in New York. Man, he wears *chains.*"

I wondered if he meant the landlord drove through snow on the way to ski. I wondered if it meant he was into bondage, S&M. That's how long I've lived with natural fibers in San Francisco. No: he meant gold chains around the neck.

The artist watched the arrival of the dawn of intelligence on my face. I capisched. Neanderthal was becoming Cro-Magnon. "Hey, now you remember him? One of your New York buddies? Don't you take care of your own?"

"Look, I hate to keep this up," I said. "I've lived in San Francisco nearly thirty years."

"Yeah, I believe you, but before that New York."

"I was raised in Ohio, Cleveland, in fact in a little place called Lakewood. Near Cleveland. But I went to college in New York."

"See? Isn't that what I been telling you?"

"And after that I lived in Paris, Detroit, Cleveland again, Port-au-Prince."

"Where's that?" he asked.

"Haiti," I said.

He paused a moment. "Hey, Gauguin went there, didn't he? The artist? But I bet you kept going back to New York."

"I visit now and then."

"So we're not arguing. We agree on general principles. It's a detail, don't mean anything. The big picture is obvious. You're from the Apple, right?"

We stood there amid the smell of sour grief, fermenting anger. The newspersons had continued delivering for a few days after the fire, so there were browning lumps of the *Chronicle*, the *New York Times*, even the *Nob Hill Gazette* like snowdrifts on the eaten front steps, in front of the smashed doorway across which an X in planks had been nailed by the landlord.

The artist caught me looking at this new construction. Nothing else had been done yet. "Okay, no consideration for the mere residents," he said. "There was a nice Chinese family with all their children and their illegal immigrants. What does Nat Grunes think they can do now?"

"A fire is about the worst thing," I said.

"Not for them. They get taken in by their relatives. And this landlord from New York, he gets to reap on the insurance, a big score you call it, and that's how it is — now your buddy gets a free run with the property."

It's like a rape, I was thinking, the destruction of a soul. We don't have roots out here, many of us, but we create our marriages or our households, our careers, our families. We learn to have an address. And then a fire cancels it out. This horror — a rape of the soul by fate, not even human malevolence — can destroy a person from the foundation. If it's shaky, if there is a jerry-built foundation, everything real vanishes and the bad dreams take over.

The ruined hulk of the building continued to shed its wet, swollen smell, attacking the nose, acid, wasted by fire and rain and secret fungoid growths, marked with fire department ribbons and signs saying FORBIDDEN TO TRESPASS. And it once contained this artist's cozy flat with his books and paintings, his things, his memories, his laboriously constructed and painfully woven fabric for passing the years, trying to give them meaning. Now gone in a swiftness of flames, axes, and water, leaving him in the street, waiting for me, breathing an alien stench.

"You're from New York, Aren't You?"

"Hey Herb, mind if I call you that? Could you put in a word for me? I mean, it's only right, this guy from New York got to make it up to me, don't he? But his kind — and I'm sure you understand how he thinks, coming out of the same stock as you do — what do they care about anybody else but themself?"

The Upward-Mobile Strippers

"I feel like a star, plus I get my exercise. I'm into getting my exercise and feeling like a star."

This was Barbie speaking, and I first met her, along with her colleague, Ken, at a premarital stag party at a spot along the waterfront, near the Marina green, which I'll call the Cortez Sailing Society. It was a celebration for a friend, a gallant liquor dealer, who was ending many years of carefree bachelordom with a carefree all-male farewell to the good old days. The event reminded me of dusty times in American Legion halls in the Midwest, the husbands gleamy and sage, the unmarried men bravely trying to hide the sadness of losing one of theirs.

Barbie was the only woman present, other than the caterers. The catering women, motherly professionals wearing antivaricose stockings, seemed in a hurry to pack up their surplus shrimp as Barbie's act began.

She emerged in a nun's habit. Some of the guests were bewildered by this apparition from their Catholic boyhoods. She raised an arm and said, "I forgive you for the sins you are about to commit." Slim and smiley Ken, bearing a tape recorder and speakers, switched on the music. Barbie began to dance and strip, wiggle and strip, pout and remove her clothes. She held little things in long, painted nails, let the little things dangle, and then tossed the little things away. Many of the guests were still sober enough to recognize that this was not one of their teachers from St. Ignatius. At least the music, to which Ken smiled and swayed, was familiar — classic ten-year-old disco.

When Barbie was down to (let's deal straight here) nothing, she began to crawl and climb across the lap of tomorrow's groom. She also slid. Her progress was slow. She began to tug at his clothes. He resisted, but her will was strong. Then Ken announced that Barbie would retreat with the groom into the back room for twenty minutes of confession.

There were cheers and hubba-hubbas.

While they were gone, Ken stated, tips could be placed in a hat he would pass, along with specific requests for Barbie's attention when she returned. Some

79

of the guests had neat ideas. On her behalf, Ken guaranteed satisfaction.

After midnight, when I left, there were ghosts rounding the running track on the Marina green, running and running in the fog-swept dark. Some people think they can sleep after heavy aerobic exercise.

When I met Barbie and Ken for journalistic drinks at the Press Club a few weeks later (we all chose grapefruit juice, hold the ice), they explained that her retreat with the groom and the passing of the hat for tips was all in fun. Barbie doesn't do any tasteless stuff. She specializes in acrobatic fun stuff. All this was — it was just a good business.

The initial style of their collaboration — Barbie's cute wiggliness, Ken's proprietary air and twitches of the mustache — made me think Ken would do the major explaining. I was wrong. Barbie was a ball of fire in the explanation department. "This is our small enterprise we have developed is what it is," she said. "Because I like acting, I like exercise, I know I got a, well, okay body, I like a can-do business," she said, "It's all in fun."

"Yes, it is," said Ken.

Ken also works as a dancer–stripper–sex object at bachelorette parties. Bachelorette? Yes, bachelorette.

"Yes, I do," said Ken.

And he also does Stripping Telegrams, according to his full-color business card, showing a well-Nautilus'd body in something like a G-string.

"Telegrams are fun. You've got to be extra careful to be tasteful and not offend anybody too much."

Their company is called Fun Stuff Unlimited. Barbie and Ken are full partners, each as full as the other. They have matching business cards and they also have dual business cards, including color photographs, first names, and service phone number. They are happy entrepreneurs. "I miss it when I'm on vacation," Barbie said, and Ken added, "We think about the future." They both have sampled the college education field and are now eager to explore the frontiers of the can-do world. "We believe in interfacing," Ken said. For example, Barbie tried nude mud wrestling, but didn't like it, even though Ken, considerate Ken, sifted through the mud first and tried to pick out most of the rocks. She found it yucchy, required a heck of a lot of shampooing afterward. She shrugged over a failed experiment. It was an example of interfacing that didn't work out.

"I'll try everything once," said Barbie.

"Most things," said Ken.

Barbie particularly likes acting. For a committed businesswoman, this is a special challenge. "Once I played the part of a pregnant girlfriend. Came into this guy's wedding party, his wife's just standing there, and I go, 'Willy, it's you! Don't you remember? What we created six months ago? Willy, you're not going to abandon me!' And he goes, 'Hunh?' and I start to hit him with my purse. . . . It was a gas. Gradually he realized this was a trick his friends were playing on him."

"And on his wife, too," said Ken.

The idea is to do fun stag things, and then sometimes fun nonstag things. That was only one skit in their repertoire. "The nice thing about being a stripper," said Barbie, "other than it's a good business, of course, is you can do it on short notice."

"If you got the stats," said Ken.

"Well, I keep in shape," Barbie said.

Indeed she does. With her, loveliness is more than a fortunate gift; it's a hobby. Athletic, agile, alert, with large, dark eyes and a sparkling smile, she is a happy body and soul, inside and out. She is optimistic and knows what she wants. Goal-oriented. Of the earth earthy. When I asked whether their parents approve, they both had things to say. "I'm a businesswoman," Barbie reminded me. (I hadn't forgotten.) "Sometime I'll either finish college" — she has done several years at San Francisco State — "or go into real estate. Probably both. I'm thinking of majoring in property management. Either that, or make this business the biggest thing in the Bay Area."

"It already is," Ken said. "Fun Stuff Unlimited. You've got our cards."

"In this field, anyway. We got a staff, we got an office, we have people answering the phones," Barbie said. "*'Fun Stuff Unlimited, Sheila speaking!'* And then she goes: 'How may I assist you?' We can pick and choose."

"Choose and pick," Ken said.

"It's acting. We get to okay our parts. We avoid what some people would call raunchy."

I wondered about their families; rewondered, actually, since they hadn't fully answered the question. Barbie looked at Ken. Ken looked at Barbie. Barbie said: "I come from a traditional-type family. They don't want to know too much. But they appreciate that I'm on my own."

Ken, the other full partner, reported that his father envies him. When Ken has an emotion, his little reddish mustache reacts. Now it was quivering, due to a small smile. "Dad's a doctor in Marin. At his age, his position, all the crazy hours he has to keep, still only makes maybe twice what I do. And I got room to grow. Frankly, he told me he'd like to be a male stripper like me."

"He looks up to you?" I asked.

Ken shrugged. Men with Ken's type of well-developed physique tend to be men of few words, small mustache.

"Ken's dad keeps in shape," Barbie said. "They've always been pretty close. He's a real flower adult."

Barbie comes of an immigrant family. Sometimes communication is a problem when the folks don't really understand that this is America, this is San Francisco, this is, what, the nineties? She is a responsible daughter. She is very conscious of the obligation to be a successful American, plus, as the eldest of a bunch of kids, to be a good example to her brothers and sisters. "Drugs are the Big Lie," she said. "I don't do drugs. Some people do. I told Sheila I'd kick her butt if she answered the phone stoned one more time."

"She promised," Ken said.

"What I do," Barbie reminded me, darting a pointed glance at my pen and pad, "I do actress-dancer-entertainer. I've been a policeperson, making an arrest in a Merrill Lynch office for, I don't know, parking tickets. Thank God It Was Friday. That's our busy day. They always get tense when I arrest them, tense when I start to strip, but then they just . . . they just . . . *laugh.*"

Barbie and Ken showed me how.

"It's a gas," said Ken.

It's the fifties, live and in business in San Francisco. Maybe it's the forties. This is a touch of the American past in our very own time, folks.

Coffeehouse Wars
in the Women's Village

"I have this terrific memory," Laura said. "I used to get A's in history because I could reel off the names of Civil War generals, both sides, Yankee and Rebel. That was grade school. I can describe every house on Fairside in Alameda. And I still remember every rotten thing that guy did to me."

"Why'd you marry him?" Timothy asked.

"I thought I liked him. I can't remember why."

Out on Valencia, in what some called the Lesbian Village, is where Timothy took his women friends who had been wronged by men. These days he seemed to be running a Gray-Spirited Line tour for the griefy. Consider the alternatives, he seemed to be saying. There were women's law firms, women's bookstores; there were women's drug counseling and child care galore; and of course all the family therapy abuse centers a person could desire. An A Capella women's chorus shared space with the Lysistrata Korean Karate & Destroy Enemy Dojo.

Not far from the Castro, with its street-corner gay men sometimes heading over to Valencia for thrift shop adventures, and on the edge of a Latino ghetto, with welfare folks of all nationalities hanging out at corners so they would be ready to deal with prosperity if it tried to sneak up on them, Valencia was developing its own bustle. The Brazilian restaurant didn't say anything about not serving men or non-Brazilians. McSushi had to change its name because McDonald's, a multinational corporation run by white straight males out of Des Moines or someplace, turned out to be McChickenshit and sued. Wall posters gave a full scientific report on the CIA responsibility for AIDS. The drugstores displayed remedies that fit all sizes.

The Diana the Huntress Café, which also sold Diana the Huntress Café sweatshirts, was a women's café. There were Amazon symbols, arrows, spears, shields, and a sun-dried copy of a book by Kate Millett in the window. Inside, there was fresh-squeezed juice and cappuccino dusted with chocolate or cinnamon sprinkles. Once again, as a demonstration of the potential invisibility of men, Timothy took a distraught friend, Laura, to the Diana the Huntress Café for her pick-me-up after their long afternoon confiding stroll.

A serving person in granny glasses, an ankle-length skirt, and a flowing purple blouse brought juice to other patrons. To Laura and Tim she brought nothing, not even conversation. "Why doesn't she serve us?" Laura asked.

"She can't see me," said Tim.

"I don't understand. You're not filmy or gauzy or transparent like some bug's wings, are you?"

"To her I am. It's the Diana the Huntress *Society* Café. It's like a club. I'm not a member."

"Pardon?"

"But *you* are. But since legally, you know, civil rights, they can't legally keep me out, they just keep me invisible."

A little indignation brought the roses back to Laura's cheeks. This was the ticket: get her out of herself.

"Should we make a fuss?" she asked.

He gazed soulfully down at the women warriors on his placemat. He averted his eyes. He cleared his throat delicately. "We don't want the pretty femme doing anything, uh, doing anything in my sparkling apple cider," he said.

"You seem to know," she said. "Then why'd you bring us here? Me, I understand, but why both of us?"

"I brought another woman here once in her deep distress. She had a sadness about a guy. It seemed to console her. You know, distraction tends to console. Smile, okay?"

She considered it. She wasn't sure she wanted to be consoled. She wasn't even amused yet. But she was just a tiny bit *interested*. "Let me try," she said.

She waved at the attractive and slender young

creature who was serving others, not serving them. The waitperson in her long skirt seemed blind; yet she was wearing her glasses. She was blind in her glasses, blinkered in her assumptions, blind to the interlopers. "She doesn't even see *me*," Laura said.

"Let me explain. You're with a man. My invisibility seems to be contagious."

"I could starve here."

"Right. We could die of thirst. Too bad for us."

It wasn't apple juice or date walnut bread sandwiches, with cream cheese, that were the issue in this territory. It wasn't even cream soda. It was politics.

Perhaps it was good for Timothy as it was good for Laura. He tasted what it was like to be on the losing side. And then they headed for a Winchell Donuts, where the orange plastic seats fit like spoons over the behinds of male and female alike, for they were all God's creatures.

Beatniks, their children, and their grandchildren gather at the Caffè Trieste in North Beach to share espresso and analyze the latest trends in poetry and conglomerate take-overs.

Commodore Ben Friedman of Postermat says he has been on duty for a hundred years, twenty-four hours a day, seven days a week. I've seen him there for at least twenty-five of those years.

The Guardian Angels patrol the mean streets where crack, muggings, abuse of the weak, sex for sale, and despair help to prove that San Francisco is a close cousin of all other great American cities.

Greg Mills (left), formerly a Marine guard at the US embassy in Managua, is now a leader of the Guardian Angels contingent in the Tenderloin.

The Mime Troupe protests and entertains from park to park. Once, when they were busted for performing without a permit, I picked up a script and began reading, but the police backed off from arresting us civilian actors.

The Mime Troupe lives on contributions — a tradition going back to the early sixties. Their rock-and-roll street theater succeeded in ending the Vietnam War.

Charlie Huy, fifty-year Press Club member and PR man, is the proud inventor of the Charlie Huy Screwdriver — vodka and, to prevent scurvy, grapefruit juice.

Street musicians don't always please everyone, for they march to the sound of their own pipes. Haight Street, shown here during its sixties glory days, is now a melting pot of upscale young couples and teenagers still looking for the Summer of Love.

The Haight-Ashbury street sign, one of the most stolen emblems in America, can be found in attics from coast to coast. These folks are letting the vibes radiate upon them.

The Ghirardelli chocolate factory, thanks to a tender-hearted investor, was not demolished, but restored into a center for shopping, theater, cafés, restaurants, and hanging out.

There are those who commute to work across the Golden Gate and the Bay — such as these gulls.

Thanks to the tradition of public-spirited rocking by both nameless and nameful groups like the Grateful Dead, free concerts in the parks are in the unwritten charter of San Francisco.

Bear and his lady are helping to mark the twentieth anniversary of the Summer of Love in Golden Gate Park. The motorcyclist's tattoos proclaim that he is a patriotic citizen of the California Republic, of which El Oso is the sacred animal.

In 1967, concerts in the parks were devoted to legalizing natural herbs and lucky chemicals or ending the war in Vietnam. Now they tend toward saving the dolphins and the forest cover. What persists is the secret subtext: here is another perfect Saturday afternoon in San Francisco, folks.

The Cabdriver
Who Didn't Want
to Be a Writer

"I don't wanna," he said.

"I can live with that."

The cabbie peeked at me in the rearview mirror. With authorial intensity he searched out signs of sarcasm, sympathy, empathy, telepathy. "Every goddamn driver in this town thinks he's some kind of artist — actor, writer, poet, dope dealer."

"I can understand that," I said.

"You goddamn well better. It's clear enough. What's your IQ?"

"Probably not as high as yours."

He jammed on the brakes on the Taylor hill. "Goddamn . . ." But in case I was a bleeding-heart liberal, he paused before he named the national origin of the culprit who had made a sudden stop ahead of him. "Goddamn ethnic drivers, they must pay off the license bureau, put in their own kind, never goddamn learn about signals, do they?"

"We're close to gridlock in this town," I said.

"So? What else is new? I thought you goddamn authors are supposed to bring fresh insights to a scene."

He was good with words. This was unequal combat. I decided to think before I responded. "I need a little space of privacy when I go into my fresh-insight mode," I said.

He considered my latest stupid remark. He wanted to make a response worthy of it. I wanted to get out before we reached the stage of intimacy and confidence where he would ask me to read his manuscript. When he cleared the hill, he said: "Always love that rose window in Grace Cathedral, gives me a kind of cathedral feeling when I drive by — that's because I'm a true poet with a shitload of unexpressed emotions —"

He smiled at me by turning his face toward the rearview mirror. He gave me a shot of winsome and helpful smile. "What I could tell a bona fide author about this town. . . . Listen up. See that garage over there on Clay? They have a garage sale there every goddamn weekend. They are professional garage sale ethnics. I bet they buy wholesale from Garage Sale Central in Stockton. They should call it Garage-a-rama. Listen, they have racks of stuff with the counterfeit labels still on it."

"I'll have to drop by," I said. "I do like a counterfeit bargain. Picked up some Air France tee shirts once, they turned out to be last year's model . . ."

"But you think they pay business tax? Nah twice over. They got juice at City Hall. This town is owned by the juice, if you get my meaning."

I almost did. He remained silent for another block. Within the period of silence he cursed a Delancey Street mover's truck. As part of his silence, he wished they would go back on dope and stop blocking the streets for innocent cabbies like himself who didn't want to be writers or dope fiends but just to do an honest American job. He gave me a short rest, though a stream of words poured out the window of his cab.

But he didn't want to leave me unattended, either. So he proceeded to tell what else was on his mind. In our local fashion, he shared. He was a man with burdens, although he had been born in San Francisco, Sunset district, with the idea of laying his burdens down. That was his mission as an infant and he had never tired of it, although these days he was a little worn out.

"How to avoid, well, in my profession, there's hemorrhoids, high blood pressure from the anxiety, there's breathing the fumes, there's like a couple-three occupational diseases. But in your profession, how do you avoid getting to be a pompous asshole?"

I gave it some thought. I was not going to be the first person to throw stones at myself. But a serious question deserved a serious and objective answer: "Just luck, I guess."

He was shaking his head. Slippery folks got into his

vehicle now and then, hookers, politicians, bookies, Colombian tourists, and novelists whose cars were in repair. I fit into this last category. But one of the jobs of a good driver is to make the passenger, who is a kind of client, a kind of customer, feel good. This is still California, after all. "What about AIDS?" he asked. "That a big problem among successful novelists?"

"I'll let you know when I get there."

"Hey, your honest comment on the situation, I'd settle for that, I'd like to get there myself. Of course, my kind of family isn't as help-their-brothers as the Establishment around here. They take care of their own. I'll bet they buy your books, too."

"This is my corner. Thanks a lot."

"Anytime, sir. Pleasure doing business with you. Ever want to read the true story of a cabbie in this period of history, here's my card. I can give it to you neatly typed. Your phone number listed, buddy?"

Beyond the Third World Lies Another World

Around the corner from the Valencia bohemia, on Mission, in a couple of blocks described by a neighborhood newspaper as the most desolate of the area — distressed by drunks and panhandlers, yet also a shopping street with babies in strollers — there is a beat-hip-revolutionary café called the Clarion, Seventeenth and Mission, where I heard a poet singing the praises of Nicaragua Risen and Triumphant. She jangled her bracelets, squeaked in her boots, and uttered her latest verses:

Ro-nald Reee-gan!
With your foot on the neck of the Nicaraguan people!

93

And we follow you . . .
Like Pavlova's dog!

After the reading, I tarried awhile to ask the poet if she meant the Pavlova who was a dancer. "And a little-known fact is she was a great psychologist, too," declared this activist, just home from her fact-finding mission.

The news made me hungry. Salivating like Pavlova's dog, I found at Country Station Sushi an easy, down-home doughnut shop decor, a bicycle brought indoors for security, salmon roe sushi, and hearty bargain sukiyaki served beneath a message tee shirt tacked to the wall. SURF USSR — the image of Lenin among a grove of typical Soviet palm trees. In San Francisco I can be not only a world traveler but a space adventurer without earning frequent-flier credits. I dipped my ikura in horseradish and soy sauce, imagining Commie beach bums riding the waves off Smolensk, singing "Ukraine Dreamin'."

This territory, Mission and Valencia, and the streets and alleys between, blend a sixties dropout devil-may-care with an eighties bagperson desperation. The mean streets are cranky; they need help from the sanitation department and the citizenry. I saw an imaginary litter box filled with paper diapers — there was no actual and literal litter box. Dogs, more curious than I am, had gotten to the pile and distributed it over the sidewalk for casual perusal. Among the prominent homesteaders in this part of the city are single mothers, along with road-killed poets, south-of-the-border nonwinners, urban Indians, junior crack entrepreneurs with skateboards, and folks on Aid to the Totally Disabled. It's clear that depression makes people feel bad. A lot of lips are explaining about their griefs to invisible companions. Vivid histories continue amid an urban decor that seems timelessly bereft. In fact, of course, people are mortal, but institutions never really die. The International Workers of the World, the Wobblies, recently still ran a unionized guitar shop in Laguna Beach, had an office visible from a place where the subway comes aboveground somewhere in New York. Deep in the bowels of Washington, DC, there must be an office and a bureaucrat taking care of the ongoing business of the NRA, with thirties recovery slogans now on microfilm. I wouldn't be surprised if some diehard Crusaders still run a recruiting tent in the deserts of Morocco. I've visited a meeting of Czarists plotting the Restoration in Paris. There's an incumbent pretender to every throne.

And so, in this place, Jack Kerouac lives, too. North Beach with its beatniks has transferred world headquarters to the Mission. The corner of Sixteenth and Valencia, with La Cumbre (generous tacos and burritos) and the Roxie Theater (no soon-to-be-on-cassette programming) and the Picaro Café and the used and unused bookshops (Marxist and feminist and gay and also books for mere reading) and the funk–punk–heavy metal–ska–reggae record companies and the painters and poets and musicians and the Mime Troupe plus the flotillas of street philosophers curing their verbal delirium by talking a lot, recall a North Beach of blessed memory. In North Beach there used to be jazz clubs, bookshops, mimeographed-poetry publishers, art cinemas; fewer of them now. But in the Mission, cheap

Mexican food fills the bellies of the settlers of the new beatnik nation as Italian and Chinese food did for their ancestor generation across town. The smells are swift and powerful. I wait in line for another supper at La Cumbre, among black-velvet fantasy scenes of Jane Russell *à la mexicaine*, tee shirts spreading the good Dos Equis propaganda, and a light show behind the busy counter where the tuckers of tacos and the packers of burritos are busy asking, "Guacamole? Sour cream? Next?" On a marquee, flashing and moving lights tell about a price increase last year. Now it can cost as much as five dollars for a dinner that makes breakfast unnecessary and may make sleep impossible. I don't know why the light show still announces an ancient price increase. The rolling tape concludes with the exclamation: LA CUMBRE!!! And then begins again.

At the table next to me an artist was explaining his technique to a visitor from Venice (California), gesturing with hands decorated with a mixture of paint and guacamole. "I try not to make any little mistakes. Concentrate on the big one is my game plan."

There are also Greek, Indian, Japanese, Italian, and Chinese restaurants, besides the cafés for soups and salads that serve those mellowing into a preoccupation with health. Aquarian ghosts arrange a high-level compromise of sprouts, tofu, and Dos Equis. Up Valencia and down Mission, women, gays, boxers, and fanatic musclepersons work out in the several gyms, clanking their machinery, smelling of the passionate will to reshape their bodies and their fates.

The bookshelves that line the Picaro Café on Sixteenth, opposite the Roxie, are shedding. The books look like Salvation Army surplus. Although they are for sale, they are also plucked out for company with coffee and muffins or the lonely bowl of soup. Many of them seem to saunter out of the café — culture belongs to the People — but others pay cash. I occasionally see the substitute mailman from my route, his uniform spotted with buttons sharing the injustices done Native Americans. I also see distributors of newspapers predicting the Revolution in English, Spanish, Tagalog, and the inventive calligraphy of various Asian languages. Around here, we don't go to pray at Mecca. We go to protest at the Federal Building.

When another Jack Kerouac documentary opened at the Roxie, the lines stretched down the block past the used-laundry, used-books, used-food, used-beer shops. This is previously-owned country. This is a territory of bedrock survival and devotion to the arts. The Monterey-jack specials in the cheese store around the corner take a person back in nostalgia to the era of gas at thirty-four cents a gallon. (The cheese tastes a little of that gas, too.) The people waiting in line to see Jack and Gregory and Allen enacted yet one more time look as if they visited a Gap boutique for instruction in how to dress downscale, beat. This is the place for the post office to recruit all its temporary hires for the Christmas season.

"You can never find one when you need him or her," said a philosopher waiting in line for the Roxie's doors to open. "But there's always a cop around when you don't want her or him."

The careful use of "her or him" reveals complex

truths about the times. Feminism and grammar can be brought to an equilibrium. The long, thin, wounded beatnik, leaning on his aluminum crutch, believed in pronoun agreement. Since he meant "one," a singular pig, he wasn't going to say "them," a plural dismissal of the guardians of the state.

"Hey," asked his companion, a young woman who eventually noticed things, "why you wearing that crutch? You get injuried at the Federal Building?"

The philosopher-linguist blushed modestly. "Naw. No. Jumped the BART turnstile at Castro and Market."

"Calcium loss," she murmured compassionately, "tends to brittle up the bones. Hey — push orange juice, nonfat milk, and, yucch, liver. If it's not against your principles." But then she brightened with a better thought. "Or shoplift calcium supplement from the health-food store."

"Doesn't he have an 'Off the Necks of the Nicaraguan People' poster in his window?"

"No, the other one. The superette. The chain. I think it's a franchise."

"You do that?" he asked. "At the Rainbow Grocery?"

"Only when I need my vitamins and it's too far to go shoplift them at the Safeway. Man, I can't spend all my life acquiring things."

He leaned on his crutch and gazed at her. "You got more surprises in you," he said, "than the suit I bought for eleven dollars at the AIDS Hospice Benefit."

This is what I mean by a road-killed poet. There is damage, but there is still poetry.

Up the street on Valencia, the Tavern Guild and

other gay self-help organizations run a permanent garage sale in a warehouse. It benefits AIDS causes. Personally, I've picked up some books there, but I tend to go to Macy's for my underwear. I'm finicky about the provenance of my Jockey shorts.

Around the corner, in the Women's Building on Eighteenth Street, on a corkboard devoted to good causes, I noticed that a restaurant was raffling off "A Romantic Dinner for Three." This feminist stronghold also houses a traditional Mission-district Irish bar, the Dovre Club, where the wars of Belfast take precedence over the Gaia Festival.

Without jet lag, without passport or visa, I can find adventure travel by taking the Muni bus. I see the world as it is and is not but should be or should not be. I suppose I'm a tourist at play here. But it's real life to those others in extremity or in outer space on the streets of Mission and Valencia.

The Sadness
of an Old Club

Because of the name, "Press Club," or, more properly, "The San Francisco Press Club," I expected foreign correspondents or literary conversation in the bar. This happens not very often. Two or three times in thirty years. Once, however, I heard a discussion of German literature. "Does Goethe rhyme with Go-Easy or Teeth?"

"Neither. *Geuu*-ty."

"You're kidding. I knew a girl named Gertie once. That's not his name wrote Go-Easy's *Faust.*"

"Wanna bet? Let's ask the bartender."

Since the bartender was Chinese, he didn't settle the matter.

When I arrived in San Francisco, kind friends offered to find me an automobile, an apartment, and a girlfriend. That's how things were done in those good old days. Howard Gossage, an advertising man who has benefited from his death by becoming legendary, also thought I needed a Club. He "put me up" for the Press Club, and I've been a member since.

The rakish black-cat symbol in paintings, sculptures, and drawings seemed to say that we Press Clubbers were prowling alley animals, but the black cat was a Gold Rush, fire, and earthquake memory that seemed to have faded into restful propriety. "A fig for care, a fig for woe" — the rhyme that greeted members — mostly applied to having a few extra drinks before the hangover struck.

The continuing edge here has been the swimming and the gym, followed by pleasant dealings with a few members who have become friends, followed far, far, *far* behind that by traditional club gang sociability. *Give me liberty* has been my motto, *but please don't give me fraternity.* In the early sixties, it was still called the Press and Union League Club, product of a merger. I was titillated by this affiliation with the Union League Club, a bastion of fine old bigots in my hometown of Cleveland. Things are different now. Bigotry is out of style. There are Asian, Latino, and black members. I used to be able to point to a portrait of Emperor Haile Selassie in a hallway. There are no Rastafarians.

The social struggle continues. Women join the Press

Club, but the nude swimming did not include them until they liberated the pool with lightning raids and legal action. Now we all have to wear suits.

The club is in trouble. The membership grows older, and new clubpersons choose to join the more yuppie-esque health establishments. The black-cat symbol, the tapestries and paintings, the traditions going back a hundred years or so, the memories of connection with the original meetings that began the United Nations do not keep members from moving away, quitting, being posted on cards with black borders. There are few press people. The doctors, lawyers, insurance brokers, and businessfolks who fill the rolls are quarreling about how to spend the money the club hasn't got.

I bring my daughters to lunch and gossip. We watch the ninety-year-old guys sleeping in the leather chairs in the library. We listen for the sound of moths eating the wool of their suits. Not much aerobic living around here. The cardplayers tease and bicker. That's Entertainment!

If the Club is not dying, it is going through catastrophic money convulsions. In the end, of course, if it convulses too much, it might die. In the meantime, real-estate solutions are being sought and past Club presidents have issued public protests, wondering if someone is taking the Club away from itself. A neighboring hotel has offered to pay for certain remodelings in exchange for certain possessions. Doubts and paranoias are treated with meetings and petitions, thus becoming paranoias and doubts. Voices are raised, fingers are pointed.

I see Ed Moose, proprietor of the Washington Square Bar & Restaurant, and ask, "What's happening?" He comes in to work off the hullabaloo of his own job as Minister of Gossip at the Washington Square Bar & Restaurant. He shakes his head and echoes William Saroyan's summary of how things go: "No foundation all the way down the line."

Years ago, in the bar, one of the members kept asking me for my card. "But you already know I'm a member," I said.

"Where'd you get those whiskers?" he said.

"Grew 'em." (I had a beard a few minutes before beards came in.)

"Bet you didn't have those whiskers when you came up for membership."

Now, after being the outsider with whiskers, I am a veteran. In San Francisco there is no strong sense of the seasons coming and going, the snows melting, but at least I can watch myself pass from being a young member to someone called "Sir." Since my sons are of college age, I no longer have to tie their shoes after our swim and steam. I can't afford to go easy on them at racquetball. Fading grandeur applies to more than tapestries, clocks, and leather chairs. I don't mind the feeling.

There are also black, Asian, and women veterans in the Club. But there is a sense of beleaguerment by the times, by graceful mismanagement, by traditions abandoned.

The various real-estate experts and advisers have been calling in their chits, and the chits have hit the fan.

This is not the place for an analysis of the merits of the case for signing over rights to the San Francisco Press Club to private hotel and club management interests. Their most recent proposal was voted down, but perhaps only this infusion of capital can save the Club. Or perhaps this action would merely postpone bankruptcy, setting up another valuable property for covetous hands. Perhaps theirs is a public-spirited interest, only intended to keep the tradition going and make an honest buck.

For some, the Club on Post Street is now mostly valuable downtown property — *real estate*. But those who have loved this shabby Press Club with its haphazard library and non-Olympic swimming pool, its cavernous bar with tattered pool tables — my sons learned the important billiard arts in this room — now are watching a slow procession of ghosts descending from the Sign of the Black Cat.

The Addict
Is Finally a Star
at His Funeral

Gathered at the Swedenborgian church in Pacific Heights, an intimate house of
worship with its old wood and warm light — it manages
to combine something Scandinavian and something
Californian — the mourners stood and listened uneasily. On this occasion it wasn't right for distant acquaintances to say, Glad to see you again.

After an appointed leader made his little speech,
sympathy to the wife and son — "I didn't know him personally but now I know he has gone to find peace at
last" — a few friends, who knew him personally, spoke
up for Freddy. A fellow painter said, "I'll bet he's happy

today. He always wanted to show in a nice place like this."

He died on the day I received a postcard from him, asking me to come to a South-of-Market gallery opening of a show of his paintings. He was an addict, supposedly clean now, but in recent months his friends had become suspicious of his behavior. He was quarreling with his family, complaining of illnesses requiring cough syrup, letting his life get away from him.

People accused him of using again. He denied it with all the fervor of a man wronged by those who loved him. There was a little-boy tone of injured pride in the denials. "Don't you trust me? Don't you trust me?"

"No," said his best friend, "I don't trust you anymore, Freddy."

Freddy fought back against himself and his past. He wanted to survive, he had a wife and son in San Francisco, he had other children back in the East Village, but if any normal trouble came his way — a fight with his wife, a suspicion that he wasn't Van Gogh or Jackson Pollock, or just the usual blahs and boredom or the kind of beat up feeling a person can get — he looked for rapid relief. Cocaine spelled relief. Heroin spelled relief. Even alcohol would do in a pinch. But what he preferred, he liked speed to get up. He liked downers to sleep. He liked hallucinogens to give him his very own head movie.

When his friends yelled, "Freddy, you're doing it again," he grew indignant.

"I have a cold, that's all."

"You have a craziness, Freddy. You're a shithead."

He looked pained. "Now we call it angst," he said.
"These days I'm an artist."

There was no meanness in him. He looked at life as
an unsolvable puzzle at his expense, but the way out of
the puzzle involved chemical dreams. Other people
make do with love, family, work, plans, ambitions. His
soul was immaculately deceived by quicker solutions.

"Freddy, you're blowing it. You're going to blow it."

Some addicts are saved. Addiction is an aspect of
the psychopathic personality; the addict uses energy,
charm, even intelligence to quell the normal notions of
how to deal with our time on earth. He's found a way to
end boredom. But it's an exhausting career to be contin-
ually in search of the next fix. When I used to ask
William Burroughs why he was an addict, he said:
"Gives me something to do."

The addict is never bored. He's always got an important task. He's moving on up to the next connection.

Which suggests an element of bleak hope. If the psy-
chopath survives into his forties, he sometimes burns
out that cool and self-serving despair. He learns to care
for others, or he may; he learns to care for himself, or
he may. The education can take place earlier, too, of
course, in such tough-love family structures as Delancey Street.

Freddy was giving it a try. He had married again, he
had a child again, he had other hopes. He thought
he might be a painter and he was working at it. When
he quarreled with his wife or the kid was a bother, he
found himself tempted. When he didn't become a star
right away, he was tempted. Sometimes he seemed to

lapse into lethargic undersea motions, swimming in a place with no known shore.

In dreams, every adolescent is a star. With drugs, a grown man can rediscover this dream stardom. When a person nods out, it's not mere oblivion he seeks. But that's usually what he finds.

Freddy found the final oblivion.

The bringing together of family and friends is essential in putting matters to a close. We might think we can mourn alone, but we can't even remember the dead properly without help. We can suffer alone, but we need to express and fulfill the suffering. Once, when a friend died far away, I couldn't go to the funeral. On that day, distracted and sad in San Francisco, I called another friend of his whom I seldom saw; we didn't care for each other; but we decided to meet at Ocean Beach and talk about our buddy. For an afternoon we were friends, too. We portioned our griefs out into little anecdotes, memories, praisings. We sat over mugs of coffee in a fogged-in sandwich joint. We remembered why we liked our pal in New York and had no need to discuss why we didn't like each other. On that day we were grateful to find another who remembered.

Now, when we meet in North Beach, we hardly speak but there is a shrug of mutuality. We shared something once.

As a child, I thought the institutions adults inflicted on us were all for the birds. I've learned how much church, temple, synagogue matter to me, and therefore can respect their mattering to others. Rituals are a form of communication; they do the work of poetry for groups. Freddy's funeral at the Swedenborgian church helped to send him on his way out of our lives and also to keep him there forever, as part of the archipelago of islands entire of themselves.

Later, back at the widow's house on Potrero Hill, their son, aged eleven, overweight, kept passing plates of goodies to the mourners. Grinning through a mouth filled with cookies, he said, "Have some more. Dad would want you to have more."

The Hunk and
the Beautiful Actress

Radiating in this house-
boat one warm Sunday in Sausalito, USA, at her ease
in a snug nook filled with copper pots on hooks and
books on shelves, a beautiful actress sat on a low bench
peacefully gazing out at the world. At first she looked a
little too perfect to be just right, but when she smiled
into my eyes, I decided to forgive her the microsurgery
on her face, the peeled gleam of the skin, the reddish
glow of hair that was not always this reddish.

At least she enjoyed the finest in the way of care. She
must have felt deep respect for others to have spent so
much time and money preparing for our meeting. She

hadn't known we were going to meet, but that was a mere detail.

Sitting by her side as the houseboat bobbed and dipped was her dress designer and companion, also very pretty, but in a more normal mode. The good sisterhood between these two women made the beautiful actress seem genuine, just folks, a politically correct angel.

We were at Gate 5 on the edge of the Bay amid a gathering of the sixties tribes for a purely social, non-revolutionary, inhale-Sunday-afternoon event. It was a houseboat warming. The whimsical but watertight structure bobbed in watery eddies and under the pressure of laughter and feet. I got up my courage to talk with the beautiful actress and she seemed relieved that someone here was not intimidated by her renown. The Sausalito houseboat set was unaccustomed to a Hollywood crowd. It was more used to bikers, artists, craftspeople, and bohemian options brokers. I said: "I really liked that picture, that was the first time I saw you, and . . ."

Although a top competitor in the 1988 Shyness Olympics, I seemed to be finding the right subjects for discussion until I happened to add — it just came out without good thinking on my part — "your leading man was a little fat for what he was doing. When he ran, he jiggled."

The skin of her face was not so tight that she couldn't frown. "I liked him in that part," she said.

"Oh, so did I, so did I, so did I!"

We came to the ceremonial exchange of cards, like Japanese businessmen; the let-me-know-next-time-you're-in-San-Francisco, call-me-next-time-you're-in-Ellay ritual. The dress designer was beaming and nodding her neat little short-coiffed head.

I was searching my mind, which had turned pure and white as the driven tabula rasa, for a fitting additional subject of discussion. Should I ask her opinion about the difficulties of attaching sewerage outlets to houseboats? How about the wars of the anchor-outs? What about saving bird-breeding grounds on the Bay?

Or something personal about, frankly, me — how I'd always admired her technique as an actress?

All that occurred to me was Aristotle, Alfred North Whitehead, and deconstructionism as a critical fashion in certain universities. This was not the moment of wit and faultless courtesy, that burst of pure charm and charisma of which other people are capable.

Well, at least I knew some interesting folks and here came one. I introduced him. Balancing a glass of wine in one large paw, my friend was moving sideways not because he is a distinguished dope lawyer and jolly good fellow with the modest habit of sliding sideways past obstacles but because he is a former rugby player who needs wide passages to get through. He is strong. He is not silent. He is solid, heavy, *built.*

"This is my pal," I said to the lovely actress.

Proudly I knitted a little group together, including the dress designer, whose name I had to ask for again. My friend the lawyer boomed out hellos in his winning way. Once I was in a car with him when a slight rear-ending took place, no real damage, a few nicks to a bumper, but the people jumped out and began making those ominous sounds about shock . . . whiplash . . .

insurance . . . you pay. He sauntered out of the car, grinned, apologized, and practically chucked them under the chins while urging them not to upset themselves on a lovely San Francisco evening. They went away happy. Standing close by, he was a powerful advocate. The beautiful actress was illuminated by the hunk style of my friend. Having completed the card exchange with me, she proceeded to discuss his belt, an Indian job he had picked up at a Cost Plus outlet in Guatemala. She not only discussed and admired it, but she ran her fingers across the fabric. "Such interesting material," she said. "Rough. Authentic."

"Glad you like it!" He is a devoted husband and father. "Hey, speaking of interesting material —" And he reached into his wallet to show her a picture of his son.

"Nice boy," she said. "But you shouldn't wear your shirt buttoned up like that." She unbuttoned the top two, three, four buttons.

"My boy's a great fisherman," said the lawyer. "We spend all our time together. Here's a picture of both of us with his salmon."

"Big, isn't it?" she said.

Hand brushing the Indian belt, then the hand running down the vast open space where she had parted his shirt over his chest, the lady said: "Tell me about some of your exciting cases. The law is one of my favorite forms of theater, it's so *real.*"

I was immobilized at this scene. I wondered if I should ask for my card back. After all, I had only printed two thousand of them and they shouldn't be wasted. The dress designer, who was also in charge of the social amenities around her friend, turned to me and said,

"Your clothes are interesting, too. No matter what anyone says, I think khaki looks good with a sallow complexion."

When I telephoned my pal the dope lawyer and hunk, I reached him on his car phone. I asked if my interpretation of what had been going on during this houseboat warming was correct and told him I wouldn't use his name.

"You're right," he said, "but you can use my name. All I talked about was my son and his big fish."

"It wasn't my imagination? She was coming on to you?"

"Hey, I'm just on my way to the Marina with the kid and the dog. Whyn't you come down and work out with us?"

On a Rainy Day
in San Francisco

"You're only half insane," a young man with his paw around a paper coffee cup was saying to another young man, "but the other half is pretty crazy too."

The once and future eavesdropper at the next table decided he was in business.

"Yeah?" asked the friend, a person with an earring in one ear, a short reddish beard, and tattoos on the knuckles of his right hand, spelling LEFT. "Well, I got news for you you ain't got for me. I've got a new lover."

A look of pain, jealousy, and congratulations passed

over the face of the person hearing this news. No doubt he wished him well, but there was that small irk of being left out in the world of romance and devotion. He said: "Tell me about him."

"Well, he's got a floor-through facing the Panhandle."

The person who had asked to be told now seemed to feel that knowledge was a dangerous thing. He looked around desperately, as if he had lost a shoe, although he was wearing two shoes, one on each foot. He was trying not to say something mean or jealous. The eavesdropper wanted to suggest he take off one shoe, then put it back on, as if he had a rock in it, to give himself something to do while he considered where the conversation could go from here. But eavesdroppers are not supposed to make helpful suggestions.

"Rent-controlled?" the friend asked.

"And plus he's had the AIDS test. Negative."

Now they were getting someplace. "What about you?"

The romantic lover shrugged and lived dangerously, lighting a cigarette. "I plan to," he drawled, "but Ah doan think Ah weel."

On a rainy autumn day in San Francisco, the eavesdropper, who was not a young man anymore but retained the habit of considering himself one, had decided there was nothing better to do this morning than to go for a walk, get wet, remember the girls and women he had once loved, find a time on the way when a cup of plain coffee could redeem all his sorrows, and then find a place to perform this act of self-indulgence.

Thus he sat in a coffee shop with his own paw around an illicit cup. It wasn't exactly a coffee shop and he wasn't supposed to be using this mug. It was the Oasis Café, at the San Francisco Art Institute on the North Beach slope of Russian Hill, and he was supposed to be drinking out of paper cups like almost everyone else, but at his age he resembled a donor or teacher or perhaps a public-spirited citizen patron of the arts more than a student. He had simply reached over and picked up a clean cup he found waiting for the relevant party. Public-spirited citizen patrons can get away with a lot.

The coffee was French roast. The milk came from a carton with the portraits of missing children on it, a Tommy and a Tammy. The honey came in a secure plastic envelope that, when he squeezed it, sweetened both his coffee and his fingers. He used water from the tea urn on his hands.

Reading the milk cartons wasn't as much fun as it used to be.

The art students had purplish hair, or greenish, or sometimes peculiarly chopped with random, semi-shaved expanses of stubble. Despite the word that high-IQ California students had given up smoking, the café was filled with smoke. The formerly young man did not wish to become crotchety with age and so avoided drawing any conclusions about these art students. Besides, beyond their dour punk or heavy-metal getups, many of them seemed to be attractively tormented young geniuses, like the ones he used to like so much and still did. Beatnik black had also come back into fashion, but it was loosely flowing Japanese black that blurred the distinction between tee shirt and kimono.

"Borrow your glasses, mister?" a smiling young woman asked.

"Pardon?"

"My film, Don't move the table, don't jiggle the tripod."

"My glasses?"

"A random effect on the lens." And like a magician she passed his glasses across the aperture of the video camera, which was regularly ticking, pointed out toward North Beach and Telegraph Hill and recording the rain. "Thanks for the lend," she said, and carefully bent over him to fit his glasses back upon his head.

No stranger had ever done this before, not this adjusting of flanges and tucking of frame behind his ears, except for those in the ophthalmological profession. This green-haired young woman was not an optometrist.

"Andy Warhol made films like that," he told the young woman. "Photographed the Empire State Building for hours, a person sleeping, a room in the Chelsea Hotel."

"He's dead," she said. "He did lots of stuff, but this is different. I'm enacting events on my video, like it's hibernating and a certain life . . ."

"Impinges?" he asked.

"I guess that's what some people might say. Randomizes."

Since the tape was running by itself, she just stood there and watched until the formerly young man made his decision. "May I get you some coffee?"

She smiled and remained as still as her tripod. But she didn't say no. He got up and started for the counter. "Black," she said. "And a pack of Kents?" So it was starting again. And for a while he would forgive everything, even her smoking. And he too had a floor-through with a view of hills and green.

Remember Uptight? This Was the Dawning of the Age of Aquarius

I stood with my friend Leo Litwak outside The Committee in North Beach, discussing New Age matters with a poet, science fiction writer, North Beach hustler, former beatnik, present hippie, and childhood member of the Hitler Youth. This last distinction often got him invited to dinner. He claimed to have been expelled for talking in class.

Now he was also a psychedelic mini-guru, wearing a long gown decorated with badges, medals, decals, and embroidered patches. Since he was a tall German with the beginnings of a belly — what we used to call a "corporation" — he looked entirely grand in his glowing, flowing caftan.

As the Broadway crowd eddied past, Leo said: "Hey, look. Interracial couples are staring at *us.*"

Our plump mini-guru commented: "Zay ahr opp-tight."

I'd heard the expression a few minutes ago. I count this occasion as the crucial pivot when the dark beatnik glooms and blahs turned into the Day-Glo Age of Aquarius. Hippie happened! The harmonic pre-convergence first got it together on that evening when I emerged from my flat on Russian Hill for the usual stroll to City Lights Bookshop, dinner at a family-style Italian or Basque place, or at the Brighton Express of blessed memory, and then to The Committee for some satirical culture and improvised companionship. On the street outside, the Jungian next door had complained, "Hey, I'm feeling uptight today."

Down the hill, John Brent, Committee actor, asked for a donation for broccoli to decorate a grave, and when I hesitated, said, "Man, all I need is about a tenner's worth. I got standards, I can't use cauliflower. Don't get so uptight."

The light was flashing. I had the honor to be present on the occasion of the birth of a cliché. Uptight was the minimum daily requirement of what not to be. Uptight, beyond drugs, civil rights, or Vietnam, was the key concept of an epoch, defining the limit of tolerance at the warm and fuzzy edge of mellow.

It was the best of times, but it wasn't the worst of times. Our hair seemed to grow longer without our willing it. At the Federal Building the cops wanted to hold us by chains like crazed pit bulls, or at least to pull our hair. Hugh Hefner contributed $10,000 to finance an advertisement urging San Francisco to secede from the war in Vietnam by means of Proposition P. He wanted no public credit, thinking the reputation of *Playboy* would just confuse the issue. Fun was in the air and in the entitlement programs. Since everyone was now a teenager, I joined the happy throng.

In a "Letter from San Francisco" for *The New York Times Book Review*, I described the new, advanced, postbeatnik rock bands that were taking on funny names, especially one that called itself the Grateful Dead. One of the band members, Pigpen, now gone to the great venue in the sky, gave me the origin of the group's name in an ancient Egyptian poem:

> *We who are the dead*
> *Salute thee . . .*

The University of Kansas invited me to read from my "Letter." When I arrived, my host said, "I'd shave off that beard if I were you."

"Is it dangerous to have a beard around here?"

"Well, it's not that we're backward, we wear jeans and all . . . " And then he looked more cheerful. "Lawrence is the San Francisco of Kansas, only we got armed guards at the gates of the university. Listen, there's a bar you can buy your acid, your grass, you didn't bring your own — *did you?* Just make sure you lock the door and pull down the shades. This doesn't make you uptight, does it, sir?"

By that time I realized that Pigpen himself composed and translated from the Coptic the poem he had quoted in a house on Page Street where we hung loose, listening to the bristly sounds of our beards growing.

Man is the story-telling animal. Sometimes we call it myth, sometimes we call it lies. We understand the difference, but don't always agree on it. During the flowering of the Aquarian Age, a generation looked to story in the form of song, myth in the form of swirling mandala fantasy, as the ways to explain a peculiar adult world out there.

Mad Alex, a tall and smiling black man, transferred his poetry creation laboratory from the sidewalk in front of the Coexistence Bagel Shop to the doorway of City Lights Bookshop. When Allen Ginsberg introduced us, Alex said: *"I got the bucket if you got the water."* For many years this has been my koan. Or maybe it's my mantra. I have meditated upon it, brooded over it, raised a family with Alex's insight echoing back during friendly evenings and less friendly mornings. Does the bucket have leaks? Will water do, or should I have brought lemonade?

Not to worry. Not to get uptight.

North Beach was crowded with street poets like Mad Alex and the Hitler Youth dropout. They didn't necessarily write down their words. They uttered them to the smoky air and depended on the faith that No Voice Is Ever Wholly Lost. The Martiniquais poet Robert Glissant calls this *"délire verbal"* — verbal delirium — and says it is a reaction of the oppressed to compression by the controlling powers.

I once saw one of these poets limping like the Tin Man out of City Lights with a stash of books up and down his pant legs and behind his shirt. He was bullet-proofed by poetry, novels, criticism, and a few magazines. I said to the manager, "I think he's stealing books."

Sadly the man at the cash register replied: "I think so, too. But he's family."

There was a beautiful young woman, married to an innovative thinker who performed light shows and invented a radar-equipped cane, who stopped me on the Kearny steps and said, "Here, have one of these."

I carried the capsule in my pocket for weeks. It was covered with lint. I showed it to a novelist friend, who said: "I like to perform experiments. I'll eat it."

A year or so later he told me he had given up novels because his IQ had gone down by twenty points, thanks to all the speed he had ingested. It was interesting news that a lowered IQ is a handicap in the novel trade. Now he does public relations.

The beautiful young woman sang with the Cockettes, danced topless, and last time I saw her was spare-changing from a doorway near the old Coffee Gallery. "Hey man, remember that good stuff I gave you?" she asked. "So give me a dollar."

With the dollar, I asked for news about her children. "One kid at Santa Cruz, one at Berkeley, and this mommy's on Aid to the Mentally, Morally, Socially, and Psycho-Metaphysically Disadvantaged. Hey, when I was dating John Lennon, you didn't think I'd be sleeping in the doorway of a bar, did you? Your pal the Bag Aquarian."

These days North Beach is more like a theme park, "Northbeachland," with only a few poets, topless dancers, galleries, and cheap restaurants to keep the faith. Like the reconstituted Pier 39, it has preserved its versions of the Eagle Café — City Lights, Vesuvio's, the Tosca, XII Adler Place, the US Restaurant, and a few newer arrivals that nonetheless fit in: the Washington Square Bar & Restaurant for advanced media folks, Caffè Sport for those who love garlic and rude waiters.

At Cho-Cho, the Japanese restaurant where Richard Brautigan liked to do his private moping, the manager once comp'd a couple their meal because, as he explained, "This lady is too beautiful to pay for her dinner."

"But I'm paying," said the man.

"You come with women who look like this, you never have to pay."

It was a more graceful way to supplement the rations than stuffing books down one's shirt at City Lights. Now things are done differently. People have to work for dinner or long-distance telephone calls. Paul Newman's stolen credit card has been canceled. The shoplifters have to contend with rude electronic buzzers. Uptight is still a sin, but grokking and grooving have sought out different terrains.

The mini-guru, the Hitler Youth dropout, was last tracked living with his wife, the Countess, in Sweden.

The Shamblers

Every neighborhood café has them, the shamblers. Let's not call them losers. Losers emanate a greedy defeat, a hopeless discouragement. The shamblers may look tired, they may have dried seeds sprouting in their beards, they may even spend the hard part of the day bent over the crossword puzzle or the horoscope section.

But when someone casts a kind look in their direction — kindness consists in being willing to listen — the light of hope comes into their faces. Eye contact causes the great disaster. They shamble over, sit down a little ahead of being invited, and with eager pride launch into their programs for saving the world, saving themselves, understanding the universe, doing good to all humankind. All humankind is summed up in their own personal, shambling well-being.

Buy him a coffee, a beer, or a fresh-squeezed juice at the Clarion on Mission or the No Name Bar in Sausalito or the Mediterraneum in Berkeley and you have a grateful friend until you die or until you ask to be excused, whichever comes first. The Mark of the Verb on the lips of the philosophic shambler is: "Hey man, you heard the real story of why . . ."

John F. and Robert Kennedy, Martin Luther King, Governor Jerry Brown, Johnny Carson, Ronald Reagan, George Bush, Honorary Doctor from a Fundamentalist College Lieutenant Colonel (Ret.) Oliver North, Francis Coppola, Dan White . . . Or any other of many subjects in the repertory of shambling rumination. "Do you know why Secretariat was shot?"

"The horse? He broke his leg."

"Nah. *He knew too much.*"

The philosophic shambler is an optimistic paranoid. He sits at the Trieste, say, and knows that he is sitting there with nothing to do because They have plotted it that way. It might be karma, it might be his pineal gland, it might be Henry Kissinger. But he's got it figured out. He has them on the ropes now.

I like to think I could give lessons in hanging out as a subdivision of the precarious art of hanging in. But there are also the risky edges in this worthy and productive enterprise of drinking coffee at the Trieste, picking up conversations at the No Name, watching the passing parade of developers and architects through the South Park Café window. Gradually a person falls prey to the shamblers. When you're busy trying to waste your own time, they come and want to waste it for you. The shamblers interrupt the private method of performing this necessary operation. They shamble up with numerological systems for winning at the track. They preach devotion to a cosmic art picked up on the bulletin board of the local natural foods. Over steaming cappuccino, which is a complete and satisfactory philosophy all by itself, better than a crystal ball for seeing the future as it should be, will be, must be — dream on, dear self, of revenges and gratifications — they waste the fumes of sincere caffeine with talk of Dr. Carl Jung.

Oh no, another Upper Grant fanatic. I thought he was cooled out with the latest visiting French student at the Savoy Tivoli.

"Hey man, have you read *The Binship Papers*? Proves the assassination of John F. Kennedy and Martin Luther King was put up by the Trilateral Commission."

"I don't believe that."

"Hey! Have you read it? Retroactive, that's how they covered their behinds. This FM broadcast lady from Santa Cruz got all the stuff on it. Over one thousand pages of *proof*, man."

"Have *you* read it?"

"Listen, I got lots to do, man, but I got a good rundown on it last time I visited my buddy in Santa Cruz.

He made it once with the FM lady, but she's more like a mother figure to him. He knows somebody read it."

Well, terrific, I say with body language and a shrug, because any spoken word plays into the hands of the coffeehouse shambler. I open my book. I take out my writing pad. I dim out my eyes.

He nods curtly and shambles over to another table to explain about the stupid closed mind over there (me). This has not been the best day for him. First the French student said, "*Fous-moi la paix,*" which means she has a boyfriend in Paris, and then he met someone who won't accept twelve hundred pages of proof.

One of my favorite shamblers, call him Arnie Moss, lives in a warehouse loft just where Valencia disappears into Market. A talented painter with a boyish smile, he has given up his art in favor of getting rich at the race-track. But he keeps his old-time smile. He has developed an infallible system. Only trouble is, it doesn't work yet because he doesn't have the funds to make the thing go. It's a *system,* see, and the operator's got to nourish a system.

"Just invest a few hundred, buddy, and I'll tell you what I'll do. I'll cut you in for a fifty-fifty share."

"My money and your genius?"

"Oh, I wouldn't call it genius," he says modestly. "Call it a God-given talent."

Then follows our ritual discussion at one of the out-door tables at the Café de Flore on Market, named for the famed café at Saint-Germain-Des-Prés in Paris where Sartre, Beauvoir, Jean Genet, and any number of existentialist postwar Americans hung out; and Arnie is nodding and smiling boyishly and I'm saying it can't possibly work and he's got the answer to that. The answer is: It *does* work. He has practiced it on paper, run it through all the tests, infallible every time, and all he needs is the good faith and the seed money that will solve the economic problems of Valencia, Noe Valley, the Castro (his boyish self). So then I say a couple hundred isn't too much these days, so doesn't he have a close friend or relative who is willing to invest in a sure thing? Someone adventurous, compassionate, deserving, and greedy?

And he says yes, he did, his brother, the dumb office manager at City College, only this one time there was an extraordinary run of bad luck, the sort of thing no one can count on — like the greenhouse effect or getting herpes from a virgin — and now his stupid brother isn't speaking to him.

I imagine Arnie's system probably has something to do with doubling his bets each race until he wins. Or maybe combining that with running tarot tipsheet cards on the horses' animas and karmas, or multiplying the weight of the jockeys by the number of kids buried at Chowchilla. Or maybe listening to the two-dollar bettors and doing the opposite on every third tip.

Arnie sails from table to table in the late afternoon sunlight at the Flore, like a treasure ship loaded with bullion, noisy with hope. The temporarily retired painter is a long, lean, youthful fellow of about fifty. He has a mop of curly hair that falls over his forehead so that occasionally young women murmur to themselves,

"Cute, cute, wonder if he's straight." When they ask how old he is, he asks them if they're numerologists, is that why they want to know? And then he discusses getting them out of a rotten nine-to-five and into the real cash by lending him some faith in a business venture involving horses. It's not risky like real estate, where you have to face irrational market forces.

That usually ends the young woman's Cute, Cute tentative decision. It doesn't matter anymore if he's straight or not.

If only Arnie's mother were alive, she'd help for sure. She always did. And she wouldn't ask how old he is, either. It was his rotten luck that she died before cryogenics reached perfection and now there's no way to thaw her out so she can invest in his project.

As the years roll on through the changeless seasons of San Francisco, this village, Arnie's curly dark looks turn a little, sort of, blondish. He doesn't dab at his canvasses much anymore, but he makes sure his jeans have a touch of dried paint on them. He's not just a mathematical genius. He has many arrows in his quiver.

"What are you doing, Arnie?" I ask when I see him bent over the columns of figures back in the smoker's corner of the Flore, where the existentialists go to cough.

"These are printouts, man, these are spreadsheets. I'm taking care of the glitches. I found a couple holes in the system, but now I got them all blocked. You want to come in for a nice fast run, settle all your economics for you?"

"Don't think so, Arnie. Hey, why are you sitting back here? I thought you don't smoke."

He looks up at me with a triumphant glare on his worn, pared-down, boyish face. "Got some serious work to do," he said, "and if I sit here, I can hope and pray the people who do nothing but just waste my time won't find me."

Tennees-mon
at the Cal Club

"**H**ey Tennees-mon, you want some juice first?"

"Ready to play," Robin said. "You're four minutes late, Mickey."

Early Sunday morning at the California Tennis Club is a quiet time, the rhythmic wet plop of the balls sounding up into the club space for lounging, reading the papers, watching large-screen color matches from elsewhere. In recent years the parking on Bush has gotten safer, but nonetheless the club has some of the feeling of a walled enclave — it *is* a walled enclave — amid the surrounding city.

When Robin first joined, accepted for membership after a teasing admissions committee interview in which people wondered just what a real-estate syndicator did (they knew, they knew), the neighborhood showed the flag of the hippies, tie-dyed shirts and blue VW vans amid the black residents. "Gentrification's my field," he had said, and a trim woman with the very dry skin of old California money asked, "Now what, please tell, might that be? Are you gentry?"

They let him in anyway. And now, of course, the hippies were gone, but the blacks were still there, plus a few gays and adventurous yuppie couples. *Gentrification* was a word even vinegared career-heiress tennis players understood.

Robin himself found a Victorian around the corner on Pierce. Since he had persuaded his wife to sign a prenuptial contract, he still owned it now that he no longer had a wife; walked to the Club; figured he'd about quadrupled his money on that house. Sure justified the dues and assessments at the Club.

"How's the week gone?" asked Mickey Sergeant, his regular Sunday-morning singles game.

"Tip-top."

Mickey shook his head. Robin gave him an advantage of exactly twenty years, but nonetheless their matches veered back and forth, sometimes Mickey's, sometimes Robin's, although Robin remembered it that he won except when he eased up or was distracted by one of the women watching from the clubhouse terrace.

"Tip-top but you won't be when I'm finished with you," said Mickey. He enjoyed Robin's elegant little Eurocisms. Once Robin had brought a guest, a developer from Montreal, who said, "*Je suis un tennisman,*" and Robin just loved it, borrowed it, modestly confided in a long-legged daughter at the bar: "French friend of mine called me a *tennees-mon.*"

"Huh?" asked the grandchild of the woman who hadn't known what gentrification was.

Not so much a Eurocism as a Canadianism.

A goddamn Quebeckism courtesy of good old Brice Godbout, who said he knew the Campeau family personally. You wouldn't think a *tennisman* could turn out to be an ordinary hustler like the ones who thought a shopping center south of Market, piggyback on the SP project, was a terrific idea.

Robin and Mickey warmed up slowly, offering each other samples of forehands, backhands, deep drives, a few lobs. After each had a chance at an overhead smash at the net, it was time to begin. Loser signed for lunch for the other; that was the routine. It was a consoling tradition in a world in which wives went away yelling, interest rates could put a fellow under, the tax code threw many a difficulty in life's path, and the humid, blond granddaughters of sun-dried admissions committee ladies started to show the signs of sun-drying themselves.

Wasn't integrity that kept them from sunscreen. Was stubbornness and a reactionary worship of bronzing.

Serve to Robin. He glanced up to see who was watching. If he didn't plan to live forever, a little leathering on a remittance granddaughter's face and chest shouldn't catch up with him.

"Take two." But he planned to live forever. "Ready."

He felt the thrill of risk, that's what tennis still did for him, as if he were a kid again and confessing he had shoplifted the flowers he brought his first serious girlfriend — grabbed a bunch from the Armenian schmuck and just ran.

That girl was as serious as they come. She giggled and said, "Hey!"

Sometimes life goes uphill from an early triumph. She smelled sweet, had the kind of even tan all over you didn't hardly see anymore, would do and in fact did anything he had in mind. He called her the Lizard. Why'd they ever break up?

Robin now knew what regret, nostalgia, lonely midnight sorrow meant to people. It was about remembering the days when safe sex, even the concept, hadn't come into style.

Upstairs, many of the women were too thin and too rich, and a few of the men were too pumped up and too rich. But a few of the women were just thin enough and the men learned, once the fad ran its course and life became real again, that pumping the Nautilus wasn't really the best for tennis. And as far as money goes, that line about passing through the eye of a needle said it all. None of these guys were camels.

"Your advantage," he said to Mickey. "I better concentrate."

"Hey buddy, concentrate your feet all the way behind the baseline."

"Oh, sorry."

The feet tended to creep up by themselves on Robin's service. You'd think Mickey would let it pass, having all the unearned advantage of age, but he sure liked to win that lunch. Mickey, kid that he was, always chose a hamburger and fries. Robin, living forever as he would, stuck with the fresh-fruit-and-yogurt, hi-pro shake.

He lost the game on his service. Okay, no sweat, not to worry. He took a stretch, a little jump. Not to watch the watchers, not to think. To play like a winning tennisman.

Anyway, the zen of tennis — Robin read an article by Michael Murphy once — said you didn't have to bear down like a stupid Golden Gate Park duffer. You just had to dream yourself into the flow of body, racket, ball, net, sweet San Francisco air . . . Then why was he breathing so hard?

Okay anyway. He took Mickey's service. Atta tennisman.

On the terrace people were pointing and laughing about the two club champs (well, not exactly) who each gave up service to the other. It irritated the zen tennisman. Mickey didn't seem to care. But it goddamn annoyed Robin.

He squinted toward them. He wished everyone would just carry on with the usual give-up and take-up chatter — giving up smoking, giving up unsafe sex, giving up, under pressure from the new IRS code, tax shelter real-estate deals. Taking up quality time with the kids, Retin-A for the skin, whatever other dumb idea came down the road. But people like to mind other people's business when the game went the wrong way. There was a silent cluster out on the terrace, and others watching from behind the sliding glass. The pretty granddaughter was sitting temporarily alone, sucking orange juice through a straw. On Sunday mornings the Club served fresh orange juice.

Maybe she needed to be gentrified. He would tell her the juice was still fresh if you ran with it from the juicer — *ran* with it.

"You really want to win this one, don't you?" Mickey said, shaking his head. It was seven-seven games again after Mickey thought he had it signed and delivered.

"Used up my minimum already this month."

"Tell you what, lemme buy you lunch now?"

"Serve, Mickey."

"How about a tiebreaker?"

"I play old rules. Serve."

Now Mickey decided to give the matter some earnest attention. There were too many people watching, folks they both had done business with, dated, didn't like to be razzed by. It wasn't really lunch or sport anymore. Sometimes this kind of mood came over a game when a person least expected it. Mickey liked to watch Robin run from left court to right and back to left, push his backhand.

It was one of those crazy hot Octobers. The hell it was the greenhouse effect, that latest save-the-whaler's noise. It was always like that in October. Robin, in his calm zen way, was doing his best to kill his opponent and buddy, and thinking that this club was the last stand of the non-sunscreen group, and wondering why the heat and distraction of the day was making this odd vacuum sensation, this unpleasant sucking, come and go.

Although his strokes were accurate, he felt there was an invisible duffer inside, pushing the racket and the ball. His breath was coming out too easily and not going in easily enough. His chest felt as if it were heading up the elevator at the Federal Building to an IRS audit.

Since Mickey was busy with his own problems, which needn't concern Robin —

Since Valerie, that was the name of the pretty granddaughter — Valerie DuCasse, might be a French name in there someplace — wasn't even watching his ground strokes, his kill —

He brought down an overhead into the net, winced, and suddenly leaned on his racket.

"What's the matter?" Mickey asked. He was panting, too.

"Is that a cloud? I think it might rain."

"Hey, Tennisman, never rains in October."

"I'm really thirsty."

"Me too. Have a sip."

"Am I being paged?"

"Are you crazy? They don't page here."

"Wasn't I?"

"In the middle of a match, Tennisman?"

Robin looked up to see Valerie DuCasse using the straw from her orange juice to pretend she was sniffing something. The young iron-pumper she was entertaining was laughing. But then both the young ones turned back around to find out what strangeness seemed to be happening down on Court One.

Robin started toward the net. "Mickey," he said. "I think something's wrong."

Letting It All
Hang Out

Hanging out on the terrace at Enrico's is where I met the lawyer who persuaded the police to return a briefcase to a hitchhiker. The kid was hitchhiking back from Big Sur, the police picked him up, and it was his favorite vinyl briefcase. Also, along with a precious copy of *Steppenwolf*, the briefcase contained $26,000 in cash.

The police claimed possible cause to suspect a crime or what they called "other illegal activity." The lawyer drove down the peninsula and said: "But it's just a briefcase. He likes it very much. And there's $21,000 in it."

"Huh?" The cop registered that. He went into the other room, looked on the shelf, closed the door, opened it again, and handed over the briefcase.

The hitchhiking lad said to the lawyer, "How much I owe you?"

The lawyer considered. It was a case for a marijuana-age Solomon. "Let's see, I had to drive south on Route One. There's gas, wear-and-tear, my time. The cop took five thousand. Okay, I'll do the same."

The boy got his briefcase back with $16,000 in it. "Hey, thanks!" he said. "That was one of my favorite briefcases."

What I seek during meals alone is curious insights about humankind and Hermann Hesse, reasonable light for reading, and fresh vegetables if possible. In my travels through San Francisco, the only places I definitely won't try, never, ever, are the ones whose proud boast, hand-lettered on the front door, reads: NO CHANGE FOR BUSS OR PARKING METRE.

I want to help them. I want to be a good citizen. But my motto, taped to my heart, is: IF NO CHANGE, THEN NO SPELLING GUIDANCE. Can't hang out in a place that doesn't give change.

San Francisco, in the area of hanging out, is generous, an amazement, and improving with time. Even Manhattan, surely a walking town, has relatively few neighborhoods for deep hanging out — Greenwich Village, of course, and SoHo and the East Village (still the land of the upraised fist, "Macramé Power!") and something in Tribeca and a bit, if you like yuppies, on the Upper West Side in the Columbus Avenue Quiche-

Blight desert and around Columbia University and in Little Italy and Chinatown and . . . Well, New York still has it. But San Francisco, America's great metropolitan village, really offers a singular prodigality of villages. Almost every neighborhood provides a café, a book place, a friendly bar, a few inexpensive restaurants — and people on the street. That's the key.

Sometimes I just need to get away all by myself to figure out why the kid with the briefcase didn't take a bus. He probably doesn't like public transportation, being a private person. I can go with that.

During the days of unlimited bus transfers, I used to climb on the Muni bus sometimes and just ride, get off and transfer and ride, get off again — stop for coffee where it looked interesting, get on again — and found neighborhoods I didn't know existed after a generation here: cafés with newspapers, gossip, lovers, real people really hanging out. Now, of course, my transfer doesn't work so well. But I'm still living off the discoveries I've made on Balboa, on Irving, in Bernal Heights, on Potrero Hill, besides my old familiar villages in North Beach, Union Street, Clement, the Haight, Valencia. Sometimes, to test my luck, I'll even head for Pier 39 to see if it's still possible to hang out at the Eagle Café. It is. Like a ragged dandelion resisting the weed killer, the Eagle Café clings to its turf. Even the witty-tee-shirt shops and softie-ice-cream eaters can't quite stifle it.

Something resists destruction in this town, everywhere except Fisherman's Wharf and what's-it, the bar where Irish coffee got started, and that pier where Scoma's is now but a bay-washed, wind-flapped seafood café was then — a place where I used to meet artists, writers, beatniks, longshoremen, cabdrivers, skilled hangers-out. The sunbathers at Aquatic Park, along with the bongo experts, made this a waterfront neighborhood for grokkers and groovers. Well, sorry; seem to have to give that one up.

The Eagle Café at Pier 39 still looks like the greasy spoon on the wrong side of the tracks where retired folks might go to complain about what the motorcyclists, at the long table over there, have done to their home place. Miraculously levitated upstairs among the fast-fun emporia, it's like a real person embalmed in a wax museum. But the scrambled-egg scrapings have the authentic burnt cholesterol taste you can find in railroad and truckstop joints in Marysville, Woodland, Stockton, Watsonville, all the toasty valleys of California and the world.

Hanging out needs to be properly defined, even in this hang-out world headquarters, where everyone seeks to be an expert. It does not mean loitering to pick up adherents of the opposite or similar sex. Does not mean searching for financial gain. The claim should not be overspecific. Should not even mean waiting for something interesting to happen.

Something interesting *is* happening. Always. This is internal business. The differentiations may seem marginal. You have to feel your way without haste. Take, for example, the Puccini in North Beach. The steam is rising in little puffs over the coffee urn. That young woman reading a book might or might not be available for conversation purposes, but the assumption must be that

143

it's a sufficient pleasure to watch how she turns the pages. Hey, she's reading. Let her read. Yeats said that we fall in love with a lady not because of her intelligence, beauty, or virtue, but because of how she pulls on her galoshes. Well, the lady doesn't pull on many galoshes in San Francisco, but she closes her eyes briefly to think upon the print dancing on her page, she jots down a note in her little carnet, she brushes the hair off her forehead. She gets a refill (coffee, not hair). That should suffice. The one hanging out has shared in the pleasure of the human machinery at peace, at rest, at contemplation, idling, at thought.

Still take the Puccini. You might go to a concert because of a specific band or orchestra, a program, or someone invited you. Here the jukebox plays what it plays. Maybe Puccini, maybe an Italian pop tenor wailing about the loss of a beautiful signorina to an American fried-chicken franchiser, maybe something from the ancient traditions of music, such as the *Chariots of Fire* theme. Whatever, the attentive hanger-out hears the notes cheerfully, follows the melody, recalls it in depth — he's been with this jukebox before.

Now take the Puccini Café some more. The drunks, wobbly druggies, and the rock-and-rollers hustle past down Columbus. The folks from Stockton to Denver with their brains tickled by strange (this is Frisco, isn't it?). The familiars of North Beach who have been here for years — who once worked for Francis Coppola, who used to bark at the topless joints, who sometimes were married to the owner of a dress shop and are now not, who read every night in the library of City Lights Books, which is unaffected by library fund cutbacks, who march primly into the latest restaurant that has not yet closed. Who also hang out. They also serve who only hang out.

Those who bend to pick up the free-soda-with-pizza fliers, the one dollar off on your SuperCut. And those whose heads are still in the stars about beatnik time, hippie time, but they're on their way to a Cheese Dog before the show down at the music joints on Broadway past the frontier of Kearny.

One night there were Animal Justice League pickets outside the Puccini, on hot information that espresso is made with meat. That's true of so much these days, but you wouldn't know it if good luck didn't happen to find you at the Puccini Café while the antivivisectionists gathered in the street, chanting, Ho ho, hey hey, let your steak and veal go out to play.

My friend Barry Oringer, distinguished film producer and writer, moved to San Francisco from Los Angeles because he likes the easy and graceful hanging out in a place not dissolved by freeways. He asked me to introduce him to this world of doing little, not much, just absorbing the evidence of the sixteen senses and the eleven manifestations of significance.

"Agreed," I said.

"Let's learn the meaning of life."

"It's a done deal," I said.

"But this week I have a script to finish, and then I'm going to Montreal to produce a film, and after that I've got to take a couple meetings in LA, but as soon as I get the development contract settled on my very personal film, then I want to call you up, hey, some evening and we'll —"

"Barry. Barry. I'm afraid we've got to start at the bottom with you. Let me tell you about the lawyer who got a briefcase back for his client who was hitchhiking from Big Sur —"

Another Slant on Telegraph Hill

Probably the only gay activist in America to have saved a prominent homophobic journalist from bleeding to death as the result of an accidental fall on the Filbert Steps — here comes the predicate to save the grammar here — is Ken Maley, passionate citizen of Telegraph Hill. He discovered Charles McCabe, who had stumbled after one of his nightly rambles, lying and dying in the dark. The *San Francisco Chronicle* columnist of drink and close shaving was rescued, and the Hill, which previously had been quarried for building sand and stone, suddenly discovered plen-

tiful reserves in its irony mines. In the curmudgeonly
McCabe there occurred a late flow of the milk of human
kindness.

The ghosts of Telegraph Hill celebrated their new
wealth. Ken Maley of Wichita and San Francisco became an enthusiastic enlistee in the ranks of heroes.

When I first came to live in San Francisco, the whir
of mimeograph machines filled the alleys. Beat poets,
hard at work in beat pads, cranked out their immortal
unrhymed rant. One particularly seductive alley offered
me an apartment where I could amble out onto the in-
cline up Telegraph Hill from North Beach, but the alley
bore the name of the wife I had recently fallen drastically
away from. Although I was trying to be practical about
things — a view of the Bay, light and air, Coit Tower
just above, and that sweet smell of the yerba buena —
I just plain couldn't find it in my heart to send my
alimony payments from an address named after that
special woman. Instead, I took a place on Russian Hill,
on Broadway, a neutral name that evoked no hectic
thoughts.

Telegraph Hill is a near suburb of Russian Hill. I
often stroll over for a short vacation. Recently Ken
Maley offered what he called "The Mainly Gay Tour of
Telegraph," providing still another vision of this lookout
minimountain and its quarried edge. We met at Malvina's coffeehouse, in the North Beach foothills, on a
sunny winter day. First we visited Washington Square,
named for a prominent father of his country but per-
versely memorializing another individual with a statue
at the center — Benjamin Franklin, perhaps an uncle of
his country. I used to take my young children to play in

this square until someone at City Hall decided the bushes that protected it from wind and traffic noises tended to make sexual encounters more private. When the bushes were uprooted, the square grew noisy and windswept. Although Frisbee artists, devoted bench-sitters, dog walkers, and public erotic explorers kept the faith, it seemed to become somewhat less hospitable. I once asked members of the Mime Troupe, which often performs here, to lead a campaign to Bring Back the Bushes now that they had brought back the boys from Vietnam.

Still, on a crisp morning, the feeling was fine. A couple was taking late breakfast from Mama's out onto the grass. The fruit salad was fresh and so was their romance. Ken led me to the non–George Washington statue and showed me where a time capsule, secreted in 1879, had been opened a hundred years later. From steel-trap memory he retrieved the woman's curious message found among the post–Gold Rush memorabilia: *"Should this modest document survive its one-hundred-year entombment, I would like its discoverer to know that the author was a lover of her own sex."*

This survival joins a stream of history of San Francisco and the cottages of Telegraph Hill that seems never to have been interrupted. When the Black Cat closed after long service to the subterranean community, places like the Caprice and the Anxious Asp took its place. The Coexistence Bagel Shop of the late fifties, near Pierre de Lattre's Mission to the Beats on Upper Grant, invited the coexistence of all races, colors, politics, and sexual persuasions. Visiting the Bagel Shop in 1957 with Allen Ginsberg, I explained to a tourist that we all ate borsch and that's why we were called the beet generation.

In the new time capsule, planted in 1979 at the feet of Benjamin Franklin, Ken Maley included seeds and a joint in order to save civilization in case marijuana had somehow become extinct. "They can smoke the joint and plant the seeds," he said, implying: And discover what helped make San Francisco a light unto the nations.

These treasures are encased in steel, lead, and a foot of cement, so don't try to dig them up in advance, dear reader.

Then we hiked up the hill to Coit Tower to visit the famous WPA murals. I've often made pilgrimage to these images of the Great Depression, the politics, revolutionary fervor, historical vision of a public proletarian masterpiece from that stalwart time just before World War II. The muggers were depicted in caps and overcoats; contemporary mugging uniform, Adidas and jeans, was not yet the rule. There's always something new to see and Ken had another discovery to offer. Near the top, in one of the panels of a lovingly detailed library, stood a book labeled Oscar Wilde. Next to it was one labeled Douglas; and then next to Douglas, another Oscar Wilde. Alfred Douglas was the famous pretty boy who got Wilde sent to prison, and so what does this library depict? Douglas between the covers of Wilde.

"Mister Ken," I had to admit, "I sure didn't notice that."

Not far from Coit Tower, he showed me the house of Whitney Warren, member of a distinguished family who headed west so that he could live his life as he wanted to live it. When the fleet was in, people used to report a trail of white, like the snow we never see, leading up the hill to this promontory. Not far from Whitney Warren's house stands the handsome cottage of Paul Smith, debonair editor of the *San Francisco Chronicle*. Both of these leaders of society lived in a day when open homosexuality caused dismay or worse. Now their houses are stops on a pilgrimage.

Ken also explained about the gardens of Grace Marchant, the Mack Sennett bathing beauty who retired to the task of building her classic park on the quarried slope near the Filbert Steps. "She cleaned out a dump. She threw old refrigerators over the cliff," he said. "We saved it for her after her death." The garden was threatened by developers, but the residents mobilized. One of the great urban spaces of America was preserved for strollers, lovers, cats. Grace is buried there beneath an ambiguous statue by Benny Bufano, his organic variation on the image of Coit Tower.

Eleanor Roosevelt used to stay in the Duck House on Alta. This low and modest residence is called the Duck House because there's an outdoor mural of, well, ducks all in a row. I learned other striking nongay facts from an ardent informer. The Flood cottage on the steps is used only once a year or so, for a party at the opening of the Opera. And the trompe l'oeil roof garden — well, see for yourself.

In the early days, these Italian fishermen's shacks were inconvenient because of the problems of getting provisions up the hill. Now they are, of course, real-estate treasures. A few years ago I appeared on a television panel in Montreal to explain how the people of

151

San Francisco have managed to fight their anti-freeway, anti-highrise wars, not winning them all, winning enough to give heart for the next battle. Telegraph Hill has been a steady winner.

We walked back down the Hill to Pier 23, passing the Fog City Diner, where my seventeen-year-old son learned one of the facts of life. We had been strolling, exploring the hill, and were ready for lunch, but the Fog City Diner demanded reservations. It was Christmastime; no room at the inn. As we were leaving, Warren Hinckle bustled through the door and I greeted the distinguished incumbent loser in the mayor's race. Then Will Hearst, publisher of the *Examiner*, emerged from his automobile and we chatted awhile. The maître d' observed these meetings. He murmured pensively: "I think we have a table for you, Mr. Gold."

"Dad," said Ari, "now I know how the world works."

I sighed. I didn't want Telegraph Hill to provide a lesson in cynicism. But lunch was served.

Mystical Doings
in the
Richmond District

Whoa! Can this be Cleveland during the Depression? In a storefront at Balboa and Thirty-fourth Avenue, Technocracy, Inc., still maintains an outpost. Not many folks now remember Technocracy, Inc., although you may have seen their practical gray Fords with the moderne symbolic squiggle on the door. The squiggle is the Monad, and it is meant to signify "Dynamic Balance."

The great flowering of Technocracy goes back to the era of the Townsend Plan. Dr. Townsend, who was a dentist, preached that a pension of $200 a month to our elders would end America's economic doldrums. Social Security stole his idea. And Howard Scott, founder of Technocracy, Inc., "is the man, the genius," according to Information Brief Number 50, "who first recognized the physical basis of social change." We're still working on that one.

So there I was on Balboa at Thirty-fourth Avenue, studying the messages and charts in the garrison window: "Reorganize the Continent. . . . A unified hydrology. . . . Come to the lecture. Muni buses go by the door." The message recalled that happy time when Science and Scientific Thinking, propagated by a fleet of gray Fords, could solve the problems of America. And here they still are, still being solved.

But this isn't Cleveland in the thirties. Next door to Technocracy, Inc., is the E. Y. Lee Kung Fu School, with its own San Francisco way of doing things: *"Creating the Maximum Performance of You."* There was a little clot of Bruce Lees–to–the–max working out inside.

And next door to E. Y. Lee Kung Fu, a storefront away from Technocracy, Inc., is the Institute of Religious Science, also called the Science of Mind, advertising lessons in "You Are Wonderfully Created." Here on Balboa in the Richmond we can find a concentration of self- and world-help labs that would be remarkable even in the neighborhoods renowned for such doings, the Haight, Mill Valley, Rome, Mecca. I also saw the tattered remnants of an earlier salvation epidemic in a bumper sticker on a pickup with a broken, annunciatory muffler: I FOUND IT.

At the Science of Mind shop, it was Mind Over

Alcohol Nite. I sat for a while at the meeting and listened to a heartfelt description of how drinking was someone's fate as it had been his father's before him, and how he could never understand just sipping a beer — chuggalug was his game — but how today he could pass a tavern without faltering. I would have stayed longer, but the pall of cigarette smoke drove me back into a balmy evening on Balboa.

These blocks swing. A couple of high-school lovers were sucking from straws in boxed drinks in front of Tim's No MSG Restaurant. The Simple Pleasures Café has an art deco (somewhat) mural of waves and mountains and creatures enjoying the waves. We're not far from Ocean Beach. This is the Richmond district, Inner Suburbia–by–the–Sea, a neighborhood of Chinese, Russian, Irish, Japanese, Filipino, Leftover Hippie, and more Chinese settlers. It's not that swift and vertical city that tourists visit, although from some places you can detect the slope of the dunes and the onion-domed golden soaring of the Russian Orthodox church on Geary.

When I visit the Balboa Theater, I usually just have coffee across the street at the Zephyr Café, but today I decided to enjoy a meal and a long loaf in this large, airy art gallery and café where New Age music was droning and calming away into the unurgent air. It almost looked and sounded like Carmel.

It isn't Carmel here in the Richmond. The last time I drove through Carmel, I got stopped by the automobile ahead of me, a fellow making a left-turn signal, his arm extended. But he didn't move. Finally I asked, "Are you turning?"

"No," he said, "drying my fingernails." I'm pretty sure he wasn't Clint Eastwood.

Leaning backwards to support a good beer-and-sausage belly, a man strolled into the Zephyr wearing red Solidarnosc suspenders. He was explaining Polish politics to the Asian woman whom he was taking to see a movie spelled, on the Balboa marquee, "FAT LATTRAC-TION." This must be the story of a husband's marital downfall, a seduction by cholesterol. The Solidarity adherent was remarking, "Lech is extorting the gov'ment to shape up or get honest, and where it ends, only Gosh knows."

A flock of young men with surfboards under their arms, coming from Ocean Beach, labored by on bicycles. A high-school couple, boy in Banana Republic surplus epaulets and girl in refreshingly non-acidwashed jeans, entered the Zephyr and ordered beer and Hawaiian Cappuccino. The waitperson stared piercingly at the boy and said, "You can both have Hawaiian Cappuccino." The lad pouted. At least they could have put the coffee in a beer bottle for him. Another young fellow, this one with spiky flattop Yakuza haircut, sullened past, his orange plastic comb showing stylishly in the back pocket of black danger pants. The Zephyr is a coffeehouse somewhat like those of North Beach, the Mission, and Potrero. Hail to thee, blithering spirits.

The serious business out here and in the Sunset is what happens when you take a community of house-loving flatlanders, traditional San Francisco ethnics, Irish and Russians and such, and bring in the new San Francisco ethnics, particularly the Chinese, who don't love their houses in the same manner. They have extended families; they want more space. They have commercial impulses; they want more value. They consider tearing down the old two-story cottage and building, oh, say, a four-story box that uses every inch of the lot and makes room for a whole bunch of relatives.

Parking problems.

Style problems.

Neighborhood problems.

It gets bitter, cruel and racial. By definition, a neighborhood in change tends to bring changes to the neighborhood. And people who like the old ways will regret their passing. And people who come in with new ways have no loyalty to the old ones.

"You put down your trailer," a hard operator said to me once in Tonopah, Nevada, "you take off your wheels, and what do you get?"

"What?"

"You get *real estate.*"

Perhaps the way the restaurants live together on Balboa provides a clue to what happens inevitably, in due course, this being San Francisco and America. The Chinese No MSG restaurants press in among the Russian, Filipino, Italian, and Just Plain Mom's places. There is a certain energy of competition. Eventually competition gives way to living and let live, piroshki and dim sum. And then you have a harmonious equilibrium once more — you find shrimp ravioli — until the Martians arrive in their spaceships and start the whole process all over again.

After my light dinner at the Zephyr Café, I was tempted to spend the next day continuing this hard work of hanging out. I drove down Geary to return to the Richmond, and the first thing I noticed was the absence of something: that thrashing big-city hustle, the perpetual heat wave jostling of Union Square, downtown. A few minutes away lies what some developer (don't do it! don't do it!) might name Richmond Village or Balboa Valley. You can almost hear the clip-clop of Rockwell Kent horses among a population of ethnic and multiracial settlers.

But this is neither Middle America nor Middle China. The French-American School stands in the cultural line down from Technocracy, Inc., and so does Alicorn, Irish Books 'n Things, which was never open when I tried to visit it, and Lion Books, also running on mysterious hours but with a tantalizing collection of "previously-read" books visible through the dusty window, and the founding center and large-print library of the National Association for the Visually Handicapped.

The Sugar Bowl, crowded with coffee-and-glazed-doughnut connoisseurs, lively with discussion and debate in Cantonese, gave me a welcoming Hong Kong energy rush when I strolled in, but once again a billowing fog of cigarette smoke drove me out. I found my way back to Simple Pleasures with its eclectic art deco, Chinese, perhaps Japanese wave-and-mountain wall painting. The slowly revolving Humphrey Bogart ceiling fans wafted the scent of coffee into every corner. A woman on a stool, doing justice to a bran muffin, recognized me for a visitor and began to explain Alchemical Hypnotherapy to me. She wasn't selling it just because she was a licensed practitioner; that was against her ideals as a licensed practitioner; she was explaining, for informational purposes only, how a licensed practitioner like her could reconcile the "inner child" and the "inner judge" that she could see struggling for dominance in my personality, and thus prevent the cancer and marital difficulties that otherwise lay in my future.

We had known each other for five minutes. When I referred to the ceiling ventilation as Humphrey Bogart fans, she corrected me: "Lauren Bacall fans."

I carried the licensed practitioner's leaflet on Alchemical Hypnotherapy to a table. A sympathetic eavesdropper in a meshed Giants cap leaned toward me to explain what was happening. "This is the new center of mysticism in Frisco," he said. "The ocean. The sand dunes. Acupuncture. Why do you suppose all the Chinese are moving in? This is a very mystical part of town."

"This is the Richmond, right?" I asked.

He gazed at me with compassion. It's so hard to make things clear to tourists from faraway Russian Hill. "This is the *outer* Richmond."

One Warm Day
at Ocean Beach . . .

I went out at sunrise. On the beach, a few runners ran, a few brooders brooded. The ghost of the Laughing Fat Lady from Playland-at-the-Beach chuckled and chortled invisibly, without a sound. I shivered, wading in the sand.

This was the same ocean I clamber along at Big Sur. This is the identical ocean of the nude beaches I used to visit during the enchanted several years of the Summer of Love. This is a different ocean, our neighborhood one. Ocean Beach lies just outside my back yard after a few minutes drive down Geary, past Chinese and Japanese villages, Cambodian villages, a Russian village.

160

The rumble of waves swept up toward the long expanse of dune. A family of fleas found my long expanse of ankle.

The truckstop, singles-stop bars, restaurants, coffee places at the Cliff House weren't open yet. I perched on a ledge alongside a man who said, turning to "Doonesbury" in his *Chronicle:* "A little political thinking sure do start the morning off right. Can you *believe* this George Bush?"

Coffee started at nine o'clock. I read the Golden Gate Recreation District explanations of what I was visiting — major water, waves, sand dunes, Seal Rocks — and looked at the Roman ruins of that crystal palace of enjoyment, the Sutro Baths, where I used to ice-skate with a German girl, twin sister of a famous actress, come to town for the Aquarian Age. I remember her mostly because she refused to cross the street against a red light, even if there were no cars. "I'm German," she explained. "It's the rule."

"You violate other rules, don't you?"

"Yah, but that's fun."

The beatnik German ice-skating twin with the stiff elbow was really a rule obeyer and the seals are really still sea lions.

At this hour of the morning, I wanted to see the sea lions, I wanted to see a cup of hot coffee. Instead, I saw the ground squirrels, which look like rats.

Finally a carved door opened and two middle-aged runners, a truck driver, a couple of tourists, and the man who began his day with political analysis from "Doonesbury" entered the café. A waitperson was chatting about her evening and I wished to hear more: "He said he was only pretending to make a pass at me when he put his head under my skirt . . ."

"Hey, maybe he has a sense of humor, you think that's what it was?"

"You had to be there, I guess."

At Muir Beach, located in the downtown center of the metropolis of Muir Beach, horses canter along the water margin. Gallant children take themselves and their animals for a ride. At Ocean Beach, in the bucolic settlement of San Francisco, a few nature lovers toke up to add to the appreciation of wind and water. A few years ago, a floating school followed a former San Francisco State teacher, who gave himself guru tenure, to a spot near the beach where he exhorted them to find the spiritual radiance within. Finally, in caravans of buses, they left California for an agricultural and publishing commune in some Tennessee or other. They live off the land, plucking tofu from the soy trees. They farm to support publication of the guru's books — one solution to the problem of the spiritually radiant writer in finding the print he deserves.

When I first arrived in San Francisco, I used to go to Ocean Beach with a clipboard to sit propped against the rock barricades, look out at the surfers gleaming in their black wet suits, and put words about elsewhere on sheets of yellow paper. It was a change from my lonely flat, where the telephone never rang, since I knew few people here. When the sun began to fry my prose, or the salt wind made me feel both chapped and greasy, I climbed the slope to find something like the White Tower flatburger stands of my boyhood in Ohio.

Now that time in San Francisco is gone, the sand dunes have swept over the Summer of Love, the Sutro Baths and Playland are demolished, and I returned that afternoon to see how the dunes and beach and ocean are making out in their loneliness. The Farallon Islands and the memory of the Castanoan Indians had kept them company in my absence.

The windmills are still stalwartly unmoved by the wind; the grayish bent trees shed their leaves in the salt-filled air. The beach was swept clean except for a few beer cans and prophylactics. There were paw prints; there were gull tracks like peace signs in the sand. I came upon a company picnic, volleyball players flopping and leaping while others confined themselves to brew hoisting. I watched, hoping to be asked to join the exercise, but they didn't need an outsider on either team. I was offered a beer instead.

At the water margin, a pair of lovers was fixed in an embrace while an older woman stood behind them with her hand on each one's back in some sort of complicated blessing. Nearby, a few hikers with packs down in the sand stood gazing out to sea, perhaps hitchhiking to Hawaii, Japan, or Bali. It's an inner-city ocean we've got out here. The percentage of tattoos on the tee-shirted men and women of the Great Highway is higher than that on, say, Union Street. The Great Highway is a great name for a great highway.

Below the Cliff House there are various promontories for watching the seals (sea lions), the birds, the ruins of the Sutro Palace. Today the seals (sea lions) seemed to have gone elsewhere and a woman said to

163

me wistfully, "Before I moved to Novato, they used to have seals here."

"They didn't know we was coming," her husband said. "Why do some people think everything is against them, even the goddamn seals?"

"I do not," she said.

I recommended they visit the Musée Mécanique (Free Admission). It seems to be a refuge of traditional delights from Playland — Take-Yr-Own Photo machines, claw candy games, Marilyn Monroe film loops, and "In the Sultan's Harem" viewing, all costing 25¢. The featured thrill is "The Unbelievable Mechanical Farm" ("Our most remarkable animated display — over 150 moving objects"), which costs 50¢. But if you're on the economy visit, you can stick to "The Great 1906 Earthquake and Fire," the "Test Your Love" machine, the plaster gypsy fortune-teller, and the mounted clippings and photographs of the heroes and monuments of this western edge of the city and continent.

The salt-rusted French-like signs help to give a sense of ancientry to the Musée Mécanique. There was no Skee-Ball, one of the ways a fellow used to be able to demonstrate his macho at Playland, and there was no terrifying Laughing Fat Lady, but I made do with the conversation of my new friends from Novato.

"How many quarters you want to spend down here?" asked the husband.

"Can't say just yet. We came all the way from Novato and the seals are on vacation, too. So let me play the Farm, okay?"

To get people to call them sea lions is a losing game, like grammar from a KCBS talk show.

Up the steps a ways, visitors were spending their folding money on beer and hamburgers in the two bars and restaurants with their flocked, luxurious, somewhat threadbare Henry Africa decor, couches, and epoxied tables, their views of sea and clouds, the excitement of drinking above the steady boil of ocean. No question, the sea air is good for the spirit, unless you happen to come from Novato with someone you'd rather have left in Novato.

Driving back past Forty-fourth Avenue at Balboa, in a neighborhood of staid houses like those I grew up with, and escaped from, in the Midwest, I suddenly noticed a row of papier-mâché monster heads lined up in front of an open garage. I stopped with an avenues-style squeal of brakes. The proud father of the monsters was giving them a bit of sun.

"Hi! Are you a sculptor?"

"What, me? No, no, I'm a chef."

They didn't look like cakes to me. I silently stated something that could be written as: "???"

"I'm a chef at the Cliff House and these are my puppets for the Mardi Gras celebration. My name is Art Bradley, sir. We have a yearly party for employees at the Cliff House up the Russian River, it's outside catered, and these are my puppets I'm putting out here to dry up for the doings."

He gave them many a proud and fond look, and showed me how he planned to paint them, and took me into the garage to show me his roommate's old-fashioned high bicycle. The Richmond-district garage-sale notices pinned to telephone poles, flapping in the salt breezes, reminded me of the old chicken-pox-and-mumps quarantine signs on Hathaway Avenue in Lakewood, Ohio, but Mr. Bradley's creations recalled preparations for the Beaux Arts ball in Paris, France. Life is not flat on the sand dunes of the Richmond, leading to the windmills, the Great Highway, and the long, rolling waves of the Pacific. On a clear day you can see Mardi Gras puppets.

Auld Lanxiety:
The Nostalgia Bars of
San Francisco

The English used to hang out at the Rose and Thistle on California near Polk, where notices near the dart board informed interested parties about the next meeting of RAF veterans, the cricket matches in Golden Gate Park, or "Smoking Drinking Hell-Raising Legal Secretary Seeks to Meet Game Australian, Preferably Male." The fireplace and general coziness attracted Anglophiles, not just English, and soon a gay clientele outnumbered the heroes of the Battle for Britain.

For a while the English met at the Pelican Inn in Muir Beach, which had the requisite dark wood, smoky

167

air, strong ales, and crinkly, crotchety pubmeister. The dart board, of course, is to the traditional pub as the popcorn machine is to the neighborhood moviehouse. At the Pelican Inn, Zen monks from nearby Green Gulch Farm provided a picturesque California touch. Five-fifths of a haiku: *The zen monk is drunk —* Now I don't know where the English go. Maybe they stay home and watch teevee like good chaps.

The French used to go to the Montmartre when it was on Broadway in North Beach: pom-pom'd sailors, wine dealers, and the music of Edith Piaf wailing and gnashing its off-key teeny-tiny teeth about the usual betrayed love. Her songs had the whine and plaint of American country-western, without any long-lost fried chicken in the lyrics. Then the Montmartre moved its jukebox and posters — Lautrec and the rest — to the Fillmore singles ghetto.

Now I don't know where the French go.

Certain hometown nostalgia bars have never taken root in San Francisco. I've asked a distinguished Milwaukeean (Milwaukite?) where the folks go to weep over sixty-seven varieties of sausage, the beer that made Milwaukee famous, the wide-bodied women of yore. "Nonesuch," he snapped crisply. "Personally, I like the Washbag." I pressed on. Once I did a term in Milwaukee and found it a city of concealed charm, culture, and secret pleasures, like all American cities. But now, when I miss the sort of people who can stand up in a bus, like President Grover Cleveland, and give three ordinary mortals a place to sit, I have no place to visit.

Nostalgia, as Simone Signoret wrote, isn't what it

used to be. I'm not prepared to hie me back to Benjamin Two to catch up on Milwaukee gossip.

The same with Cleveland, my hometown. I was born there in the cradle of poets, the lake country — the Great Lakes in this case. Out on Clement or over on Potrero Hill, in Cow Hollow or down in the Tenderloin, even as far away as Tiburon or Fairfax . . . I fail to find that cozy corner where the Sweet Singers of Cleveland gather on a Saturday night to talk about the Indians, University Circle, and the singles bars of the Flats, where a fellow can hear the most authentic Dixieland this side of Erie, Pa.

The beatniks-*en-retraite* have theirs: Vesuvio's on Columbus in North Beach, where "we are" — still — "itching to get away from Portland, Oregon," or Spec's XII Adler Place. The Anxious Asp, owned by Bunny Simon, used to be a beatnik joint in North Beach, and then it moved to the Haight where it became sort of a hippie bar (but hippies didn't drink), so Bunny — a handsome Creole from New Orleans — started selling Creole food until the city closed out that enterprise for plumbing and kitchen problems. So then he ran the Anxious Asp on behalf of those nostalgic for the good old days of black-white boy-girl meetings, a class operation like everything Bunny does. But these days it's permanently gone — for the time being.

I can't imagine a psychiatrist's bar. Angelo Quaranta's elegant little restaurant on Russian Hill, Allegro, attracts a few psychiatrists for casual shoptalk — "Hey, remember when you didn't have to fill out all those stupid Medicare forms?" — but despite what my mother thinks, a restaurant that serves wine is not really a bar.

Veteran ballplayers used to go to Lefty O'Doul's. At least people who knew batting averages went. And journalists still gather at Hanno's in an alley near the Joint Operating Agreement. A subdivision of the beatnik-hippie group still hangs out at Gino & Carlo's in North Beach, where Charles McCabe used to take ten minutes from his drinking to write his column. This is the Fighting Artist set.

The first time I visited Gino & Carlo's, I headed for the Gents' after a beer and was politely stopped by a young woman playing pool with her nearest and dearest male friend. She extended her mouth with an unlit cigarette in my direction in the mute appeal known to all.

"Sorry, I don't smoke," I said.

"Well then, fuck you," she said.

Finishing with my business, I returned past the pool table to find her friend beating her to the ground with a pool stick, shouting, "How many times do I have to tell you to watch your language? Don't say 'fuck you' to a goddamn visitor!"

I ran to the bartender and said, "Aren't you going to do something?"

"They know each other."

"Lemme call the cops."

He looked at me with disdain. I was not a Gino & Carlo's veteran. "They don't come in here, buster," he said.

The CPA bar doesn't exist to my knowledge. In the Mission there are Latin bars, often still decorated with shamrocks — more about that in a moment — that serve steam table food, and where I once overheard a semantic discussion of America's drug problem. "It says here in the paper the drug czar is gonna take on the cocaine kingpin."

"Whazzat mean?"

"It's czar against kingpin. What the hell kind of democracy is that?"

On my way out, at the corner of Sixteenth and Mission, I threaded my way through a group of kids selling the Muni Transfers That Time Forgot. I had learned something. When Central Americans come to the United States, they don't want an authoritarian regime. They want to be arrested by plain folks.

Now the Dovre Club, pronounced either "Dover" or "Do-vray," incongruously located in the Women's Building off Valencia on Eighteenth, that's a genuine Irish bar. It doesn't need a shamrock decor. IRA sympathizers gather in this cool, damp, beer-smelling cavern. Irish-American journalists who run for mayor conduct their campaign out of the Dover/Do-vray Club.

But isn't it a little superogatory, *de trop*, unnecessary to get into a description of an Irish nostalgia bar? When you're Irish, shouldn't every bar be yours by right?

Here's the part where a member of Abstinence Anonymous makes his prognosis concerning the nostalgia taverns of the future. Singles bars, both straight and gay, still exist, but the times seem to be pushing them toward the mauve area of historical resonance.

(Okay for Harry's; okay for Perry's; no need to take up collections yet.) People are not drinking enough to support the rents of Hong Kong landlords. There is little nostalgia to be found in the paper-bag dreamers of South-of-Market doorways.

Guy Haines, the distinguished veteran master-of-revels at the Templebar — a somewhat Tiffany resort for downtown office workers — recently took a step heavily freighted with significance. He got married. At his stag party at the Golden Gate Yacht Club on its windswept promontory at the Marina, a lot of old friends thought it was the end of an era. The man who had everything now wanted something more — a wife.

Ah! There's the hint of permanent nostalgia, more persistent even than the San Francisco shamrock taverns and the signs with that martini glass outlined in purple neon. The formerly-married bar. The one for those remembering better times or worser — a resort for those nostalgic for that old nostalgia of theirs. "My bar or yours?" When they were happy or sad and now can't quite remember which.

Christmas
of the Losers

Watkins wandered with the other ghosts in North Beach on Christmas Eve — the divorced, the bereft, the deserted, the left-out. Better to be a footloose ghost than a drunk and fancy-free, he decided, although not yet convinced about how he would end the night with sleep.

He tried the door of City Lights Bookshop, but it was locked for the holiday, the staff having a family glass of wine and waving him away through the glass. Watkins wasn't of this family.

He tried the Caffè Trieste, also about to close. Red and green wrappings lay strewn about, along with spackles, the snow that was a necessary part of the decor here in San Francisco, too, where it never snowed. The noisy good cheer of the Trieste reminded him of the quiet dignity of the upright codgers taking the turkey special at the Big Boy. Everyone, like Watkins, was trying hard. He moved on up Grant, heading against the chill currents of damp, invisible fog gusting down the slanting street. The last Christmas sellers were giving up; iron grills clanked; soon the Store for Rent signs after another inadequate season would open the street for next year's hopeful merchants.

"Yo! Watkins!"

"Pardon?"

"Turn *right,* man, how many times I have to tell you?"

It was Rodney, the laughing black sociologist from the Hoover Institute. He liked to balance his ideology, formerly Reagan, now moving on up to Pat Robertson, with some of the street style of his brothers. As far as he was concerned, the estrangement all came from the brothers and he was ready to make peace and tell them how to do right, as he did. "You be alone like me, hey man? I got a party for both of us, plenty for everybody, this rich lady live up on Stockton. She just *love* horny intellectuals. "

"Do I qualify?"

"Almost, but one in seventy-two adults in the Bay Area pass the state bar, man. That's the statistic. Merry Christmas, brother." The sociologist came close and peered earnestly into Wat's face, a streetlamp gleam coming off the steel rims of his glasses. "Nothing happening on this pre-holy day?"

"Nothing much." Watkins had a reputation for telling the truth. It helped him to stand out in the crowd of one lawyer per seventy-two adults. "So how I beat my Christmas depression is I give in. I like to have a good long sweaty walk, a hot bath before midnight, and so to bed, like Tiny Tim."

"I bet you do," Rodney said. "I bet you really prefer a long cold walk, a long hot soak, and then down to your pallet on the floor, alone, where nobody can bother you to rub her back or things. I bet."

Wat shrugged.

"Listen, this is a party, kind of. You're invited." Rodney, a compassionate neoconservative soul, took Wat's arm, took no no's for an answer (Wat didn't bother), and steered tightly. "There'll be cold turkey and hot possibility, brother, plus all the nice people just as wrecked as you are this holiday season. Being an honest man, I include myself. . . . Hey, remind me again about Tiny Tim, would you?"

The door was unlocked. It has a little card Scotch-taped above the knob: UPSTAIRS. COATS, CARES, & WEAPONS IN BEDROOM. MERRIE XMAS ALL.

Wat and Rodney strolled into a room lined with three long couches and knees bumping off them. A turkey was being escorted toward a low driftwood coffee table, already equipped with plates of cole slaw, cranberry sauce, Italian breadsticks, and sliced canned beets. The hostess and cook remarked by way of greeting, "Hi, I'm Sheila, move the ashtrays."

"I'm Watkins," Wat said, "thanks for having me."

"I said, *Move the ashtrays.*"

The other guests, seeming paralyzed on the

couches, hadn't jumped to help. Wat, seemingly paralyzed by the sudden crowd, couldn't understand a direct command. But sharp, high-IQ Rodney moved the ashtrays, beamed, and said, "*Voilà.*" He also helped to lower the platter. "Um, good-oh, we're just in time."

"You're welcome," Sheila said. "You Watkins the public-interest attorney?" She wiped her fingers on her apron and then extended them. "I'm happy and proud to meet you at last. Called your office to offer a class action suit against the purveyors of sugared coffee, I suspect it's more sugar than Gourmet Viennese Roast, and all I got was the brush-off."

"Must have been one of the associates," Wat said. "I'd remember if I talked with you. They shouldn't take that responsibility, but after they pass the bar, that's how they are."

"If it's more sugar than coffee," she asked, "shouldn't it be sold as a sugar product rather than a coffee product?"

This kind, generous, intelligent, good-looking in the slightly over-the-hill way that Watkins, at his stage in life, even preferred . . . this good-natured, hospitable, perceptive lady was one of those legal nags. The medical nags corner the doctors: Hey, I got this persistent ache in my left ear when I drink herbal tea; what do you do for a scaly ankle, Doc?; all my family dies of the sugar diabetes, think I should give up Mars Bars?

". . . but we never did the lab tests," Sheila was saying, "because your office wouldn't give us the time of day. If it's forty-nine percent coffee, do we still have a case?"

"I'd love to hear from you during office hours," Wat

said, "really. Trouble is, on Christmas Eve I can't think of litigation, not even General Foods."

"Goodwill toward mankind, huh Wat? And a multinational corporation is legally an entity, a human being? You're a kick, Wat."

"Thank you. And it's good of you to sort of invite me."

She waved to the platter. "Have some turkey, white or dark. Sue if I don't provide the color you prefer."

Those sunk into the three couches began to stir, vibrating a little as their motors idled, and then, as they realized they didn't run the danger of being absolutely first in line for the meat, began to push and jostle at the platters of food. Soon other platters arrived. A slow sighing filled the room. On this Christmas Eve far from childhood, there might not be love, family, trust, connection; there might be an absence of solid holiday cheer; but there would be enough food. Two jugs of wine, one white, one red, stood flanked by little bottles of high-fashion water. The gas of the fireplace hissed. Some of the men were wearing sweaters with that woolly bulge over the gut. Some of the women were wearing sensible pants suits. It was cold outside; steam on the windows. The rumor that San Francisco took part in sunny California was not confirmed by the evidence.

One woman caught Watkins's interest. She was long and bony, with interesting, sharp planes in her face and a shiny gambler's vest over a white blouse. Lean and rangy, he thought, and wondered why someone wasn't crowding those skinny knees, that coltish body. Her hair was carelessly major — hand-tousled. He could imagine her taking off her glasses and a man in the movie saying, "Why, you're beautiful!" But she wasn't wearing glasses, only the slightly gleamy look of contact lenses. She didn't invite him to her with a glance. He went anyway and she smiled when he said, "Merry pre-Christmas, why aren't you eating?"

"I was waiting for someone to ask."

So he took her elbow and steered himself and her to the table. She picked a very small amount of everything in a way that suggested she didn't want to waste and wouldn't necessarily be finishing even these small mounds of white meat, mushroom-and-walnut dressing, cranberry sauce. With her fingers she added a sprig of parsley from a water-filled bowl.

"Hey," Ferd was saying — he was a North Beach coffee merchant with both retail and wholesale outlets, but the wholesale outlet had been closed as a by-product of his divorce — "hey, we could all be buddies in times of adversity like Frank Sinatra, Dino Martin, and" — raising his voice as he glanced at Rodney — "Sammy Junior Davis, in times of adversity or other, like a modern-day version of the mouse pack —"

"Davis Junior," Watkins murmured, unable to avoid correcting the errant liberal.

"Only the first of several problems with what he stated," the lean, rangy lady, Beatrice, said. "Rats. Rat pack. He's been studying ancient history." Her smile was wide and ungoverned by the look of the sort of woman who selected the party pack of winsome smiles in a mirror. It was an old-fashioned grin. It blew away the whiff of schoolmarm and made her seem younger than her actual, oh, maybe thirty-eight years.

"Hey, that's nice," he said. "You're a corrector, too."

"Only the first of *my* problems," she said. "I like you, also."

He hadn't said he liked her — but if he had, would that be a problem? But she was reading him correctly. "Are you always a little ahead of people?"

"I'm always a little out of sync. For example, back when —" A rosiness appeared in her cheek. She was blushing! And she plowed right ahead with what was about to make her blush. "Back when nobody was wearing a, wearing a bra . . . I wore one."

"I noticed."

"How could you? Didn't know me then. But now I don't — do things in my own time."

"That's what I meant I notice."

"Oh." She laughed. She said nothing. She let the blush fade and then appear again. And then she buttoned up one of the buttons on her blouse, leaving the top two as they were.

He noted the gesture, he let her know about the notation, he let her wonder whether he would let it pass. He let it pass. He liked the hang of her shiny gambler's vest, some kind of find from the Barbary Coast Antique Clothier. "What is it now," he asked, "nineteen eighty-nine or so?"

That was his way of letting it pass. He didn't expect any answer. He had grown rusty at party banter. But he kind of liked this Beatrice, liked her as much now, when she was going toward lean and rangy — had gotten there already — as when she might have worn a bra to a Christmas Eve get-together for those who didn't go home for the holidays. It would work with plump and it worked with lean and rangy, this one.

There are always some who can't go home for the holidays; no money; don't want to; no home to go to.

"You two have plates," Sheila said, peering into each of their faces, making her own estimate of the preholiday situation, "you have food in your plates, silverware, at least one of you is showing a napkin. But you're not eating."

"Hey, we're getting organized."

Beatrice dropped to a step leading toward the door and Watkins sat alongside. First he tried to put the plate on his knees; that didn't work so well; then he tried the floor, but it was too great a bend and reach. Beatrice was laughing at him. People were jostling around them. He didn't like shoes so close to his turkey and fixings. Beatrice was still studying him and laughing about what she had learned. "Not used to partying much, are you?" she asked. "Normally a loner, are you?"

"Normally an eater at tables," he admitted grimly. She was delighted. The smile wouldn't quit.

The light in the room was yellow and warm. The people were not talking very much, pending the start of wine-fueled jollity, but there was a busy clash of teeth and silver. This helped. It was the noise of ice being broken. Sheila's house was filled with things, souvenirs, posters, Season's Greetings propped on mantels, not a menacing rich woman's house. In a corner, on a pedestal where a person might expect a sculpture or an Egyptoid lamp, stood a complex bit of machinery with jagged teeth on its snout and the message on a plaque: *Oldest Orange Juice Squeezer Known to California.*

And alongside Watkins was sitting an attractive, not too beautiful woman, the warmth of her flanks communicated to his flanks. He should surely be feeling better about life. And having successfully argued the case for felicity against himself, he suddenly did. Feel better.

"You don't have any olives," he said. "Let that lack be remedied."

Beatrice plucked a black olive from his plate, and neatly removed the pit from her mouth with the same fingers. She was easy with him and easy with herself. She didn't demand that life bring her only pitless black olives. Surely all this suggested a promising situation for a lonely divorced male. She had reached into his plate as if she belonged there. If anything can be slightly aphrodisiac to the parties concerned, it's the ameliorating by good luck and a bold reach of the normal holiday depression. "That's the case," he said.

"Pardon?"

"I think aloud sometimes, even when I'm talking with people."

"Nice, Wat. A little controlled schizophrenia is a very attractive quality in a man."

"Maybe you better run that by me one more time."

They were good buddies already. They joked. They sat very close on the carpeted step. They were the envy of everyone, although Sheila looked only half-envious. Her pride in the art and craft of hostessing compensated her, or perhaps it was only that she didn't really find Watkins her sort.

"The law of averages," Kenny Jones was saying, too near to them, meaning to be overheard, "someone at least in this room has AIDS or Syndrome."

"The law of averages also states," Sheila remarked,

her patience as a hostess beginning to be tried, "we'll all be dead in due course. So let's be careful. What else're you trying to suggest?"

He shrugged. "Just small talk like anybody else. It's on my mind."

Reassuringly Sheila leaned over and patted Watkins and Beatrice, in turn, on the shoulders. "Don't you worry. I'll vouch for both of you, especially you obey safe practices. Let me get you some carrot and celery sticks, picks up the immune system, just in case."

When she turned away toward other guests, Watkins asked, "Are we doing the right thing?"

The cool, gray eyes of Beatrice — long eyes, lean eyes like the rest of her — widened. "What are we doing?" she asked.

Now he had shocked her. Certain things you say and certain things you don't. He was unskilled in the matter of Christmas Eve flirtation. As at any time, desperation is the wrong way to go.

"Talking only to each other," he said. "Perhaps we're rude."

"Good recovery," said Beatrice. "Way to go." She took another olive from his plate, another black one, and again removed the pit from her mouth with the same two fingers. "Let's not decide if we're going to spend the night together till later. Then we'll poll the jury."

"Have you had legal experience?"

"Neither a plaintiff nor a defendant," she said, "but I keep up with my reading."

They had gotten past that tender point in the discussion, the moment when a person might go to get a drink and forget to return. He didn't know for sure if they were just joking. He wasn't even sure of the legal status of the term *just joking.* On Christmas Eve, far from home, or maybe no real home, perhaps certain rules were suspended, like alternate-side parking. He saw the point of food, drink, music, and other people in such situations. It gave a legitimate reason for distraction. A person could fall silent and still seem to be paying attention.

"Your place or mine," she said so loudly that, two bodies away, Kenny Jones jumped.

Watkins was ready to admit when he was wrong in both small matters and large. He had predicted she wouldn't finish her plate. She had eaten methodically through the little mounds — creamy slaw, vinegary slaw, turkey, cranberry sauce, dressing, other festive stuff, and finished with the parsley. She looked up at him, grinning, a bit of parsley on one tooth, and said, "Aren't you going to finish? Too nervous to eat in company?"

"Do you mean it?" he asked.

She frowned. She picked the parsley out. She tried to give him an answer. "People needed to do this back in the sixties, didn't they?" She put an olive pit back into her mouth, giggled, and removed it. "Nervouser than you can imagine."

"I like that about you, too."

"Do you shoot people? Are you a pervert? Are you an emotional mess?"

These days all that had to be covered. "Not for me to say. But I'm not in a risk group."

"Well then," she said, "it's Christmas Eve and there's got to be room at the inn. Let's be on our way."

Falling silent, the other guests stared, chewing turkey, sipping wine, as Beatrice and Watkins went for their coats. It wasn't a true silence. It was a kind of reverent hum. Sheila stared over the edge of a bowl. It was how she liked her coffee. She had the rights of a hostess and householder to her own large coffee bowl. Beatrice and Watkins hurried down the stairway. This wasn't France where a person had to shake hands good-bye with everybody. This was America, where things can happen suddenly.

Friendly neoconservative Rodney stood swaying at the top of the stairs, holding a paper plate piled with slaw. "Bless you anyway, Tiny Tim. Just remember you owe me now, is that agreed?"

One Foot in Light
at San Quentin

Its magnificent site on a curve of the Bay makes developers flush and turn pink with desire. A person can see condominiums in the mind; if he is so inclined, a person might imagine the storied walls and flowered quad of a small college. But San Quentin is a hard-core suburb of San Francisco.

I used to visit the prison as a member of the San Quentin tennis team — a group of writers competing against inmates — and none of us had ever played against such honest and gentlemanly line calls. But then came George Jackson, riots, murders, and the prison was locked down tight. Now, after being checked for felonies in my history and being warned not to wear blue jeans, so as not to be confused and confusing among the prison population, I was invited back to a Saturday night at the theater.

I even brought a date.

Samuel Beckett's great and mysterious play, *Waiting for Godot,* in a production by actors and a musician at San Quentin, should have been a triumph. A Swedish director worked with the actors. A film team, preparing a documentary about the eighty-three-year-old playwright, was taping the performance. An audience of Bay Area actors, critics, writers had passed the various tests, metal detectors, and body searches to fill the seats in the San Quentin gymnasium. Barney Rosset, Beckett's close friend and American publisher, had flown out from New York.

But that day a friend of the actors had hung himself. There had been an epidemic of suicides at the prison; there usually is. One of the actors was so depressed and sick that he could barely lift his head when we saw him before the play started. Honored places had been marked out up front on the board seats for the family of one of the actors. They were expected to come from Los Angeles, from Watts, but it turned out that they didn't manage to find the money for the trip.

And the performance was a triumph anyway. The man with a depression and a blinding migraine headache rose to the event. The man whose family didn't show up played with piercing simplicity and force to the empty seats and to everyone else, his lonely cries echoing with both his own and Beckett's lament for an endless waiting. The enactment, and the concluding sweet sounds of the flute, lifted the audience to bravos and an ovation that didn't stop until the guards ordered the prisoners back to lockup, the guests out to their cars.

We could see Mount Tam, edged in moonglow. I read what Spoon Jackson, who played Pozzo, wrote in the program: "As human beings, we all have one foot in light and one foot in darkness."

Waiting for Godot was first done at San Quentin in 1957, by the San Francisco Actors Workshop. Since then, a play-tracking satellite probably would have found it performed in some language, someplace, every week of our lives. Prison actors doing it have come out to make careers for themselves; a San Quentin veteran, upon whom the Nick Nolte movie *Weeds* was based, now lives in Paris as an interpreter of Samuel Beckett for the theater.

When I asked Hampton Finney, the classically trained flautist who played the music for this production, where he found the haunting melody that concluded the show, he said, "I learned it from a tape." It was a Yugoslavian pan-flautist and composer's work. I told him he brought tears to people's eyes and he said: "I play gospel, too."

James Bennett Wells, enacting Lucky in this production, is a Vietnam veteran with a wife and six-year-old daughter in San Francisco. I didn't ask why he's at San Quentin. He said about Lucky, who is a slave with a rope around his neck, guided by a whip and shouted commands: "Lucky is lucky because he has a job, a purpose in life. He's not among the unemployed."

Donald Twin James (Vladimir), Happy Wilson (Estragon), and Danny K. Leffel (The Boy) all spoke of loneliness, faith, pain, suffering, their own lives and the life of the play. Danny Leffel is small and blond and needs protection in prison; he *looks* like a boy. Donald James wrote in the program about Vladimir: "He's a guy who is after something . . . searching for some type of freedom which, at the moment, he can't find."

Neither can Donald James. All these men are waiting, Samuel Beckett is waiting, and we in the audience are waiting — so is everyone. Perhaps we can share the burden of waiting, but not compare its weight for us with its weight for others.

The editor of the San Quentin newspaper looked familiar. "Haven't I met you before?" I asked.

"I've been in twenty-six years," he said.

I had talked with him when I played tennis with the gentlemen of the tennis team. Since then, I'd been married, had three children, been divorced, and gotten on with my life. Since then, he had stayed at San Quentin.

Since then, the prison has gotten tighter. Tennis with outside visitors has disappeared. I came to the gates of the prison once for a "literary cocktail party" in honor of publication of a book of George Jackson's letters. It was the time of radical chic, when a lawyer who was later shot by one of the men she tried to help could cry out: "All prisoners were political prisoners!" Then there was the shoot-out. There is a memorial stone to murdered guards in a walled space, set with flowers and well tended, oddly reminiscent of a college quad; except for the towers and guards, of course.

After the performance we were able to chat briefly

188

with the actors. They were striving to be artists and succeeding in bringing new life, their own lives, to *Waiting for Godot.* Probably most of the visitors had that familiar thought: Why are they in prison? These are seekers, these are human beings.

And then someone pointed to a window. "See that room there? Third from the right? That's Charlie Manson."

We didn't have to look far for despair and madness. There were needle scars on the arms of some of our hosts.

Jan Jonson, the director who had come from Sweden to work with the players, described their lives, with an understated mildness, as having "an uncertain future." Spoon Jackson, who played the violent Pozzo, wrote in a poem that, two years ago, he knew nothing of poetry, but now:

> . . . *the dark clouds roll in*
> *nourished yes created*
> *by the sweet waters of the sea.*

Privately, so as not to embarrass the actor, a collection was taken by some of the visitors so that the family from Watts could fly up to catch the last performance. Perhaps it was an appropriate Beckett irony for the actor to wait in doubt until the last night in order to see his family in the audience. In Samuel Beckett's universe, he'd have waited in vain, but this is America, isn't it?

The Summer of Love
Will Not Go Away

Healing a troubled spirit after some difficult times, I used to take my daughter to Sabbath services — it was more like a festival of meditation — at the House of Love and Prayer, on Ninth off Irving. This was a real house, it was a home on a street of coffee shops, natural-food stores, a neighborhood hardware; and here dwelled ecstatic Jews who believed in dancing, singing, and the guitar, in addition to traditional rituals and prayers. On Friday evenings, after sharing the silences and songs, the experiences of connection with God, a group dinner was served. Sitting down together to share food is an essential part of the connection.

There was a family warmth for which I was hungry. I held my daughter's hand; she held mine. A leader of the group stood up to make a little talk filled with parables and blessings, speaking with that chanting tone in which mystic statements take on the rhythm of questions. "And so what did Dov Baer, the Magid of Mezeritch, say are the three things we can learn from a child, the seven things from a thief? He *said*. . ."

The leader that evening was an awning maker by profession, a Chasid by vocation. My former wife said she hadn't known about Chasidism, just as she hadn't known about awning-making Jews.

Yes, some Jews are mystic dancers, guitarists, and awning makers. Even a venetian-blind specialist could be found on Irving Street.

Among those who partook of the roast chicken, potatoes, and salad, the parables and the prayers, were two single mothers with part-black children. One was Norwegian, dramatically leaving the Arctic Circle behind her. The other was a young woman from South Dakota. Both had been flower immigrants to the Haight when the Children's Crusade swept over San Francisco. In her charming Norwegian accent, Ingrid said, "I departed my family forever, my son is neither black nor white, so now I think maybe we're Jewish."

"I used to see you at performances at the Straight Theater, didn't I?" I asked, and she blushed happily: "Right! Right! But I don't think so."

She was in stringent need of a new history as I was

in need of connection with an old one. The House of Love and Prayer helped us both.

Alas, I don't find the House of Love and Prayer in the telephone directory anymore, but there are Chasidic groups all over the Bay Area, attracting the young, the mystics, and the needful. This should include just about everyone. But as my own difficult times were made more normal, I drifted away, remembering with gratitude this oasis off Irving Street that linked an ancient teaching, nurturing, and celebrating tradition of Judaism with a new California style. And I remember the wise awning maker in his woven skullcap.

Another tradition hangs on — the San Francisco free rock performance in Golden Gate Park. It needs to be called performance, not concert, because of the sharing of an implied history and vision. Also, people stand up and wiggle. When I heard that Big Brother and the Holding Company were appearing at the bandstand in the park one warm Saturday (of course it would be warm), with a singer described as "the new Janis Joplin," two decades were wiped away. In San Francisco, that seems as long ago as the days of Dov Baer, the Magid of Mezeritch.

The music soared and the singer had a powerful and expressive voice, without the gravelly ruin that appeared in Janis's sound toward the end. She rocked good, like a white girl should. But it was the crowd that provided the extra edge. During the lecture about Greenpeace, the dolphins, freedom of the ocean, the sentient beings of the deep — Greenpeace was sponsoring the event — I visited among my fellow music lovers. They were also, like the dolphins, deeply sentient creatures.

Giant Hell's Angels, leaning on their hawgs, had not roared into the park to save the dolphins from the tuna fisherpeople. One Angel, stripped to the waist, with acres of bear and dragon tattooed across his back, down to the cleavage, noticed a camera pointed at him, put on his mirrored sunglasses and his camera look, and stared with professional menace into the lens. He doesn't do windows, but he does ominous pretty well. Then he turned, like a lamb on a spit, to make his portly back available for a different angle.

"Do you shoot color?" he asked Gene Anthony, official photographer to the Summer of Love.

Burnouts, bikers, and unregistered tenants of the park hung out on the edges of this scene, but being a Hell's Angel in the company of your tattooed moll means you never have to be lonely. You certainly don't have to say you're sorry. I wondered if the bikeress with the twisting-crocodile swastikas on her cheeks might learn what they mean before she was thirty, might regret them at forty. ("Hey, I wasn't no au pair girl, you know?")

An editor of the *Weekly Freak,* published in Stinson Beach, passed out copies of his paper, a collage of appeals on behalf of the homeless, reviews of the "Electric Bash Re-Union" at the Kennel Club on Divisadero, and news of the hero who, in the line of duty, fell off the Golden Gate Bridge during his protest happening to celebrate the handicapped and the elderly. Thanks to being a superrelaxed protestor, he survived — somewhat shook up.

Scoop Nisker, free-form radio champion, beatific, taped interviews for his show and said again and again, "She's the new Janis Joplin. Isn't she great?" He too often wears a woven cap and does his best to master the scene by celebrating it.

An ancient LSD dealer, now a graphic designer or a pensioner or something, called out to me, "Hey, you old whippersnapper, what's been happening?"

"The last twenty years? Been going to the movies, how about you?"

"Caught a good one the other night. Man, have you seen *The Unbearable Lunches of Being*?"

Evidently his electric mind perceived the film as a story about the bringing of blintzes and kasha to Prague. I used to know him when he urged the cooking of the buffaloes in Golden Gate Park, because this is meat that belongs to the People, and then he had become a vegetarian. Brain damage was making him more original, but by this time I was interested in a new friend.

Big Bones, a slick and handsome man, performs his blues-revival act for passersby at the corner of Fourth and Market — bringing the tradition of the blues to the commuting masses — and also indoors at the Milestones Club on Fifth Street. ("Big Bones and His Bone-a-Fide Blues Band, Raphael, Joe, Mark, and Sir William on Vocal," said the flier he was handing out. It was more than a pizza-with-free-soda flier.) He has a bodybuilder's physique, which a person doesn't necessarily expect of a blues artist, and he also works as a weight trainer. He used to have a straight job as a middle manager for a textile company in Reno, but he didn't like Reno — it's not the most soulful corner of America — and he prefers to sing for the folks in his hometown at the corner of Fourth and Market until better things come along, such as the Milestones Club. "It's the tradition of my people, the blues," he said. His enunciation was very precise; his style was cheerful. "I like the happy blues, but I know about the other kind, too."

"You were raised in the Fillmore?"

"We called it the 'Mo, those days. I can't say with all honesty I grew up with rats biting on me. But we had to think about the money. I'm of this generation, thinks about the money, and this generation still needs the blues."

We paused to listen as a Greenpeacer finished her amplified rap, the whistles and cheers began, and the new Janis Joplin rolled into another mighty number. Big Bones was beaming. He wasn't jealous. The more music there is, the more music there is.

An elderly couple was peeking at our conversation. When normal late-middle-age hearing loss sets in, eavesdroppers start to compensate with lipreading — another example of the glory and indomitability of the human spirit that William Faulkner celebrated in his Nobel Prize speech. I asked if they often came to concerts in the park. "No, this is our first — we drove down from Seattle," said the husband.

"We parked our new Honda Prelude in a crosswalk — do you think it'll get a ticket?" the wife asked.

"If it does," said Big Bones, "you can sing the blues, too."

Something in the sun and the air, the children of

hippies in Air Assault high-topped basketball shoes and making peace signs, the Hell's Angels looking for photographers with plenty of color film, the folks saying, "It's a gooood day" — that two-syllable *goo-ood* — all this experience of living history made the elderly visitors from the northland of rain and Boeing willing to risk a towaway of their Honda Prelude loaded with all the options. It was a return of that famous San Francisco weather — good vibes. "We heard Frisco used to be like this," said the wife from Seattle.

"Still is, still is, sister."

Big Bones gave them his flier, inviting them to Milestones, or, if they preferred the economy tour, the corner of Fourth and Market. If I could find it again, I'd also like to invite them to the House of Love and Prayer. In San Francisco, in America's great metropolitan village, in the nineties, those who don't always know they have troubled spirits are still seeking their own Chasids and blues-revival singers.

You're doing good work, Big Bones.

And one of the seven things a thief can teach us, according to Dov Baer, the Magid of Mezeritch, is: If you don't find what you need one night, try again the next night.